The Home Front
Britain 1939-45

Clive Hardy

iNostalgia

The Home Front
Britain 1939-45

(Above). Merlin engines receive a final cleaning before testing at the Ford shadow factory at Eccles. (*Daily Herald*).

(Opposite page). S160 type heavy freight locomotives for the United States Army Transport Corps (USATC). On arrival in the UK, 174 were allocated to the GWR, 168 to the LNER, 50 to the LMS and six to the SR. After the invasion, those S160s used in the UK were refurbished prior to being sent to Europe. (*Daily Mirror*).

Clive Hardy

ISBN 9781845472559

Published by iNostalgia, 355 Wilmslow Road, Fallowfield, Manchester M14 6XU

Smiles all round as the first of six pairs of knickers are made from an old night dress. 1941. *(Mirrorpix)*.

Contents

Introduction

Welcome to The Home Front, Britain 1939-45, an illustrated account of how the greatest conflict in human history impacted upon the everyday lives of the people of the United Kingdom regardless of age, sex, medical condition, social class, religious persuasion or any other label you might imagine.

2020 marks any number of anniversaries associated with the Second World War. The seventy-fifth anniversary of its end as well as the eightieth anniversaries of the fall of France; evacuation of the British Expeditionary Force from the beaches at Dunkirk; the Battle of Britain; the blitz on the city of Coventry from which a new word entered the lexicon of warfare – Coventration or the destruction of a city from the air – are but a few of them.

The photographs have been selected from the Mirrorpix Archive, a vast collection of newspaper images dating back to 1903. Making them available to the public is an ongoing project, many of those selected for this publication having only recently been uploaded to the Mirrorpix website. All I have done is flesh out often brief, and in some cases incorrect, captions. That captioning was sometimes incorrect is no one's fault as some had been heavily censored. Others were the victim of newspaper practices. During an event, a photographer takes multiple images. One is chosen for publication by the picture editor and captioned. However, all the other images - regardless of subject - are sometimes filed with the same caption as the published image. It has been great fun unravelling it all.

One of the problems when compiling a book of this type is being confronted with a mountain of superb photographs, many taken by photographers who never received a credit. Wherever possible I have attempted to track them down though, alas, the photographer diaries have long been consigned to the dustbin. Even so, there are some truly outstanding images. Thankfully, many taken by George Greenwell, Bernard Alfieri, and John Heddon of the *Daily Mirror* were traceable. Armed with a 35mm camera, George went out at the height of the London blitz on the night of 11 January 1941 to record for posterity some of the most atmospheric images I have come across.

One, depicting two firefighters in Tabernacle Street, was later turned into a painting by George Campbell and features on the dust jacket of the *Blitz Then and Now Volume 2*.

This book is divided into sections, opening with The Lights Go Out, a brief look at the Czech Crisis, Munich, and the inexorable drift to war. This is followed by Civil Defence, simply due to the timeline as Air Raid Precautions kicked off during the second half of the 1930s. Then we have Operation Pied Piper – the evacuation programme beginning on 31 August 1939.

Following on, we have The Home Front, Fed and Watered, then Entertainment and Sport. These are followed by Industry Goes to War, The Blitz, and finally Victory and Beyond, a look at the postwar period and how the war would cast its long shadow into the 1950s.

Just a word about price and measurements. Prices are given in £. s. d. followed by the decimal equivalent. To put them into perspective, I have also included the 2019 equivalent based on the Bank of England's inflation calculator. Doing so brought up some interesting figures. For a 1930s vacuum cleaner on sale at £40, the 2019 equivalent is £2884.30p, and that £4648 is the 2019 equivalent of a £100 fine in 1944. Measurements are given in imperial units followed by their metric equivalents.

This is not an academic work, nor is it a definitive account of those years. What it is, however, is an attempt to recapture the atmosphere of the period through images selected from the Mirrorpix Archive and the archives of Reach regional titles including the *Birmingham Post & Mail, Bristol Post, Liverpool Echo, Newcastle Chronicle & Journal, Manchester Evening News, Derby Telegraph, Reading Post, Swansea Evening Post* and the *Western Mail*. Above all, this is a book designed for dibbing in and out.

All that remains is for me to thank the following people, some alas no longer with us, who over the years provided help, information, or inspiration to delve into this period in our country's history. Ada England; Joan Nisciel; Michael Nisciel; Tom Richardson; Nancy Richardson; Joyce Stanley; Alton Douglas; Jo Douglas; Gordon Stretch; Bryan Barton; Nigel Arthur; Russ Brown; John Low former editor of the *Derby Evening Telegraph*; Mike Inman, Chris Ward and Tony Attwater, my former colleagues at the *Derby Evening Telegraph*; Richard Felix; Cyril Sprenger; George Black; Pat Otter; David Tilley; Vincent McDonagh; Claire Beal; Geoff Ford; Malcolm Smith; Fred Mabbott; Jim Wright; Tim Rayment; Betty Korsak; Frank McNought; Nicola Joules; Ray Simmons; Mike Howden; Jill Crowther of Hull Local Studies Department; Arthur Credland of the Hull Maritime Heritage Centre; Paul Harris; Ralph Gee, former librarian *Nottingham Evening Post*; Bryan Raynor of Swan Hunter; Neil Hadkiss, Des Cannon and Jackie Haynes of the *South Wales Evening Post*; Keith Scrivener of the *Plymouth Evening Herald*; Natalie Jones of *Mirrorpix*; and finally, Malcolm Pheby, who drew the short straw and had to edit this. Please forgive any omissions.

So welcome to what was, and what is, the Home Front, Britain 1939-45.

Clive Hardy.

A V1 flying bomb, also known as a Doodlebug or Buzzbomb, on display in Piccadilly, London, in October 1944. In some early Press reports they were called robot bombs. *(Newcastle Chronicle & Journal)*.

The Lights Go Out

The German annexation of Austria in March 1938, followed a few months later by the Czech Crisis and Munich, were enough to convince most people in the UK that war with Germany had become a matter of when, not if.

The Czech Crisis came about following a speech made by Adolf Hitler on 20 February 1938, in which he promised protection for all Germans living outside the Reich. The speech was seized upon by the Sudeten Nazis in the ethnic German areas of Czechoslovakia. Hitler, on something of a roll since the annexation of Austria, backed the Sudeten Nazis.

France was bound by treaty to aid the Czechs if attacked. British policy toward the Czechs was ill-informed and unsympathetic. The French feared that, in the event of war, Britain would declare neutrality and keep out of it. Anglo-French conversations during the unfolding crisis were publicly portrayed as the two nations working on a joint policy to resolve the matter when, in reality, they were about abandoning the Czechs to their fate and at the same time preserving French honour. British diplomatic moves consisted of hinting to the Germans that we might intervene, whilst positively discouraging the Czechs from fighting on the grounds that we most definitely would not be intervening.

Events culminated the following September at the Munich Conference to which neither Czechoslovakia nor the Soviet Union was invited. Despite the French sabre rattling, the conference was little more than a sham. Britain's Prime Minister, Neville Chamberlain, was determined to cling to his policy of appeasement, persuading Hitler to sign a document that Britain and Germany would in future settle any differences by negotiation. The outcome was that Hitler gained everything he had wanted and, at the same time, had destroyed France's military credibility. Also, he had successfully isolated the Soviet Union and

Air raid trenches being dug in Kingston Gardens, London, 27 September 1938. What few anti-aircraft guns there were – predominantly World War One vintage 3 inch (though new 3.7 inch weapons were in production) - were trundled into position and balloon barrages flown at a number of cities.(Alfred Markey, *Daily Mirror*).

Poland, and inflicted a diplomatic defeat upon Great Britain. However, Britain's Prime Minister, Neville Chamberlain, had averted war. He came home to an albeit brief hero's welcome.

Interestingly, evidence exists that at the time the German armed forces were in no fit state to fight a war. The rapid expansion of the German army had resulted in a serious shortage of officers and experienced NCOs. Some units were untrained, there was only six weeks supply of munitions and fuel reserves stood at just 25 per cent of mobilisation requirements. On 1 August, the Luftwaffe stated it needed at least eight weeks to bring its strength up to a respectable in-commission rate and, even then, training and flying hours would have to be slashed. More worrying was that reserves of some aircraft lubricants stood at only six per cent of the mobilisation requirement. Thanks to their superb propaganda machine going into overdrive, Germany's bluff was never called.

In October 1938, the German army occupied the Sudetenland and the following March the land grab was completed when what remained of Czechoslovakia was absorbed into the Reich. With 35 divisions and tanks far superior to anything the Germans could put in the field, the Czech army would certainly have given a good account of itself.

The Czech Crisis tested Britain's readiness for war. Air-raid trenches were dug in parks and what few anti-aircraft guns there were in the country were trundled into position around London. Balloon barrages were flown at London, Plymouth, Portsmouth, Manchester, Glasgow, Newcastle, Hull, Sheffield, Birmingham, and Coventry.

On 24 March 1939, Britain and France agreed to resist any German aggression against Belgium, the Netherlands and Switzerland. The following week, Britain joined France in guaranteeing Poland's borders. Poland had previously signed non-aggression pacts with the Soviet Union (1932) and Nazi Germany (1934).

Neville Chamberlain returns from his meeting with Adolf Hitler and waves his now famous, or infamous, 'Peace for our time' note. *(Daily Mirror)*.

The real threat to Poland came when the Nazi Party gained control of the free city of Danzig. The Poles had seriously considered launching an all-out preventive war against Germany but had refrained when Britain and France refused to get involved. Hitler, inspired by the inability of Britain and France to get their act together, decided it was time for Danzig to be returned to the Reich together with access to the city across Polish territory. Poland rejected the demand out of hand.

On 20 August, the world was stunned by the news that Nazi Germany and the Soviet Union had signed a trade agreement. Three days later they concluded a non-aggression pact, together with a secret agreement, to carve up Poland and the Baltic States.

As the international situation deteriorated, Parliament was recalled from its summer recess on 22 August to "meet on Thursday next, when the Government proposes to invite both Houses to pass through all its stages the Emergency Powers (Defence) Bill." Only eleven members of the Commons voted against the Act that had the potential to bestow unprecedented and wide-ranging powers on ministers and senior bureaucrats alike. Defence Regulations could now be issued as Orders in Council without recourse to Parliament.

Any violation of a Defence Regulation was deemed to be a strict liability offence punishable by fine, imprisonment, or both. In theory, the regulations held precedence over all other laws, including Habeas Corpus, as offenders could be detained indefinitely without trial. Under some regulations, the prosecution no longer had to prove guilt "beyond reasonable doubt." Anyone unfortunate enough to be hauled before a court was guilty as charged unless they could prove their innocence. Various regulations also introduced unprecedented powers of stop, search, and interrogation as well as the automatic right to enter premises without having first to obtain a search warrant from a magistrate.

The only safeguard against any abuse of power by the executive was the fact that all Orders in Council containing Defence Regulations had to be laid before Parliament at the earliest opportunity. Once laid before them, both Houses had twenty-eight days to scrutinise the Order and, if necessary, either House could resolve that it be annulled.

American help with the growing Polish crisis was requested. However, United States Ambassador Joseph Kennedy's reporting of the situation gave the impression to Washington that Chamberlain was attempting to force the Poles into unilateral concessions, when what he wanted was for the Poles to state they were willing to negotiate. On the international stage, this would put Hitler in the wrong if he attacked. Also, if Hitler chose to negotiate, the Poles ought to be able to drag it out long enough for the winter rains to make invasion all but impossible until 1940.

Originally, the invasion had been scheduled for dawn on 26 August, but the previous evening the Italian dictator Mussolini informed Hitler that Italy was not yet ready for war without massive military aid. That same evening, Hitler met with Britain's ambassador to Berlin, Sir Neville Henderson. Hitler told him that he was prepared to guarantee the British Empire and would approach London with an 'offer' once the Polish question had been settled. On the evening of the 28th, Hitler took the diplomatic initiative by asking Henderson, "whether England would be willing to accept an alliance with Germany?" Henderson exceeded his instructions and replied that 'speaking personally' he did not exclude the possibility provided that "the development of events justified it."

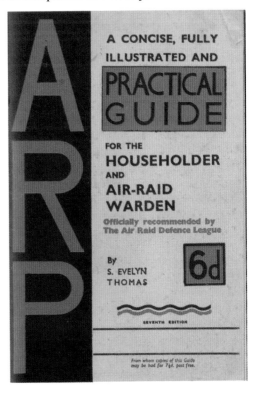

A CONCISE, FULLY ILLUSTRATED AND PRACTICAL GUIDE FOR THE HOUSEHOLDER AND AIR-RAID WARDEN

Officially recommended by The Air Raid Defence League

By S. EVELYN THOMAS

6d

SEVENTH EDITION

From whom copies of this Guide may be had for 7½d. post free.

Unfortunately, Hitler's moderate tone was interpreted by London as a sign of weakening resolve and he would buckle if brought to the negotiating table. The following evening Hitler played his ace. He would negotiate providing a Polish emissary arrived in Berlin by noon on the 30th. Hitler was convinced the British would agree to an alliance and that two possibilities would then arise.

Firstly, the Poles might refuse to negotiate in which case Britain would be justified in revoking their treaty obligations. Secondly, if talks went ahead and then broke down, Chamberlain could refuse to fight on the grounds that the Poles had provoked war. To his credit, Chamberlain was too wily to fall into such a trap and informed Cabinet that the demand for a Polish emissary was unacceptable and any Anglo-German agreement depended upon a just settlement for Poland backed by international guarantee.

At 4 pm on the 31st, Hitler had had enough and ordered the invasion to take place at dawn the following morning. Polish aggression would be the excuse. At 8 pm, a German radio station in Upper Silesia was attacked by Polish troops, only the troops were convicted criminals promised a reprieve if they took part. After the attack, the convicts were executed, and their bodies still clad in Polish uniforms were left for the local police to find. Radio stations in Eastern Europe were soon broadcasting that Poland had attacked the Third Reich.

At 4.40 am on 1 September, the German battleship *Schleswig-Holstein*, moored in the port of Danzig on a friendship visit, opened fire at close-range on Polish fortifications at Westerplatte. An hour later, German armoured units crossed the Polish frontier and the Luftwaffe launched raids against Warsaw, Cracow, and other cities. At this late stage, Britain, and France, using Mussolini as an intermediary, said that they were still willing to negotiate providing German forces withdrew. Hitler, anticipating a short, sharp war of no more than two weeks, refused.

On the afternoon of Saturday 1 September, the King held a Privy Council meeting and signed the order in Council, ordering the complete mobilisation of the Army and Royal Air Force as well as a proclamation ordering the mobilisation of the Royal Navy. The Defence Regulations came into force at sunset and would last for 2061 consecutive nights.

At 7.30 pm on 2 September, Chamberlain appeared before the House of Commons. Members on both sides expected to hear that an ultimatum had been delivered to Berlin. Instead they were told that negotiations could still take place if Hitler withdrew. Chamberlain sat down to a silence that was deafening. Not a cheer, no applause, just deafening silence. The acting Labour leader, Arthur Greenwood, rose to his feet. Encouraged by members of all parties, he spoke. "Every minute's delay now means the loss of life, imperilling our national interests…imperilling the foundations of our national honour." The House rose in confusion.

The ministers Hore-Belisha, Anderson, de la Warr, Colville, Dorian-Smith, Stanley, Wallace, and Elliot, met with Sir John Simon. Later, Sir John and a group of his 'mutineers' met with Chamberlain and told him they would no longer co-operate with him until war was declared. At last, Chamberlain spoke. "Right, gentlemen, this means war." The Cabinet met in an emergency session at 11 pm.

At 9 am Sunday 3 September, an ultimatum was delivered to Berlin. Two hours later it expired without reply. At 11.15 am, Chamberlain spoke to the nation on the radio. He told his listeners that his work for peace had failed, that the Germans had not responded to the ultimatum and that "Consequently this country is now at war with Germany."

Just twenty-five minutes after the declaration of war, the air-raid sirens sounded their ominous warning over London. People in the streets calmly made their way to the nearest shelter. It was a false alarm.

Hurricane Mk 1 fighter at RAF Northolt, 1938. *(Northcliffe Newspapers)*.

Members of Merseyside ARP try out their full decontamination suits. 8 December 1938. *(Liverpool Echo)*.

Esher AFS put their Coventry Climax trailer pump through its paces during a civil defence exercise at Sandown Park, Coventry, in April 1939. (Bernard Alfieri, *Daily Mirror*).

Civil Defence

The establishment of Air Raid Precautions arose out of Cabinet approval in 1935 for the spending of £100,000 (approx. £7,211,000 in 2019) on planning for the contingency of war. It was widely expected that aerial bombardment would start within hours, if not minutes, of war being declared. A direct result of the Munich Crisis was a massive surge in ARP recruitment so that by the end of 1938 it stood at 1.4 million.

Most ARP members were Wardens, whose job would entail enforcing the blackout and then using their local knowledge to access the extent and type of damage so the Control Centre could despatch the appropriate rescue services. The Warden was also responsible for getting survivors to a shelter or Rest Centre. The Senior Warden was recommended to make a large informative map of his area. Some of the information to be included was the locations of factories, garages, hotels, schools, and cinemas. Also, first aid posts, pharmacies, doctors, police stations, fire watch posts, and hand-firefighting equipment. All water supplies including fire hydrants, emergency water tanks, canals, streams, rivers, ponds.

All places where a member of the public could take shelter in the event of a raid. The map was to be hung up in the Wardens' Post, and, if possible, a copy given to each Warden. There were normally six wardens to a post, and one post for every 500 people. More than 90 per cent of wardens were part-timers, and one in six was a woman.

The Control Centre was responsible for directing First Aid Parties and Rescue Men. First Aid Parties consisted of four men, an ambulance, and a driver. All were experienced first aid workers having been trained by either the Red Cross, St John's Ambulance, or the St Andrew's Society. Their main task was to assist the Rescue Men in releasing trapped casualties and then administer what aid they could. A decision would then be made as to whether a casualty needed further treatment at a First Aid Post or hospital. First Aid Posts (FAPs) were usually manned by a trained doctor, a trained nurse and nursing auxiliaries. There was normally one FAP to every 15,000 people.

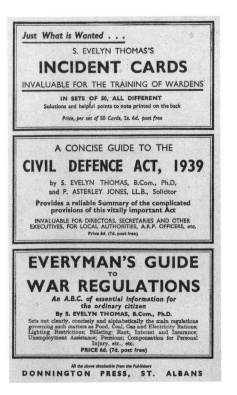

The task of the Rescue Men was the real back-breaking work in Civil Defence. Often amid fire and with the ever-present danger of explosion from fractured gas mains, they searched the debris for both victims and survivors.

The threat of gas attack was taken seriously and ARP drills in which gas masks had to be donned became regular occurrences. In certain circumstances, householders were advised to select a room, basement, or dry cellar for converting into an airtight, gas-proof and splinter-proof refuge room. The most important ARP work was preventative as in evacuation and the use of shelters.

Special duties devolved to the police, special constables and the Police War Reserve including control of air raid warning systems, liaison with the military, billeting of soldiers, preparation of military routes, piloting of army convoys through towns and cities, photographing prisoners of war, anti-invasion preparations and security duties.

The Women's Voluntary Service for Civil Defence was formed in 1938 as a branch of ARP, its initial function to inform households on how to protect themselves and their community in the event of air raids. There were no ranks. The WVS was split into twelve Regions conforming to the same geographic areas as the Civil Defence Corps. Members made bandages, swabs, and hospital clothing in large quantities. During 1940, the WVS launched a major recruiting campaign for staffing Rest Centres. Sheffield alone enrolled 1600 women by December.

Auxiliary Fire Service

In the 1930s, though many towns and cities possessed highly professional fire brigades, these brigades could not be expected to answer all the emergencies resulting from a major air raid. The answer was the Auxiliary Fire Service (AFS). The Fire Brigades Act, 1938, allowed regular brigades to increase their establishment of men and appliances, and, because of the situation in Europe, recruiting began for the AFS.

AFS equipment usually consisted of trailer pumps towed behind suitable vehicles. They were manufactured by Coventry Climax, Scammel, Worthington-Simpson, Beresford, and Dennis. The pumps came in a variety of sizes capable of

delivering between 120 gallons (545.5 litres) and 900 gallons (4091.4 litres) of water per minute. Pumps were either single axle with the power to pump the water supplied by a four-cylinder petrol engine or of the four-wheel variety with the power supplied by a Ford V8 engine. The smallest pump, the wheelbarrow pump, required just one man to manoeuvre it and was designed to be operated in confined spaces.

The AFS had two basic self-contained fire appliances. Most were based on a Fordson or Leyland chassis and equipped with a Sulzer pump capable of delivering 900 gallons per minute. The second type, known as the 'extra heavy', was again based on a Fordson or Leyland chassis but equipped with a pump capable of delivering 1400 gallons (6365 litres) per minute through six jets or branches. AFS fire appliances were painted battleship grey and lacked the brass and chrome adornments of regular machines.

On 30 August, all AFS and regular units were issued with steel helmets and respirators. The Home Office announced that weekly rates of pay for full-time personnel would be £3 (£197.57p in 2019) for men, £2 for women (£131.71p in 2019), £1 5s (£1.25p) equalling £82.10p in 2019 for youths aged 17-18 years, and £1 (£65.68p in 2019) for youths aged 16-17 years.

Trench Shelters

First made their appearance in public parks during the Czech Crisis. At the beginning of the war, the Government ordered local authorities to make these shelters more permanent by lining the sides and roofing them with concrete or steel. Trench shelters were unpopular as they were often impossible to keep dry.

Public Shelters

Surveys were carried out in town centres to assess how many existing cellars and vaults could offer some protection to the public in the event of air raids. Local authority buildings, shops, pubs, banks and so on were pressed into service. Brick and concrete public surface shelters were built and, though similar in design to 'communal' surface shelters, they could accommodate many more people.

Shelters of this type often gained individual characteristics and some sort of social life developed – often with official support. Concerts, play readings, libraries, and communal sing-alongs became regular features. The larger public shelters had full-time wardens and were equipped with their own first aid posts.

Surface Shelters

Introduced from March 1940, these were communal. Constructed from brick and concrete, they were designed to accommodate up to fifty residents from a street or block of flats. However, because of a cement shortage, many early examples were built without mortar thus making them liable to collapse if hit by the pressure wave from a bomb blast. Ventilation was limited and, even when chemical toilets were provided, they could be unbearable. There were also sandbag surface shelters.

Anderson Shelters

Named in honour of Sir John Anderson, the Anderson shelter was a familiar sight at the bottom of many a garden and thousands of examples still survive eighty years after the start of the Blitz. By the end of October 1939, approximately 2,250,000 Andersons had been distributed free of charge, but a change in Government policy resulted in those earning more than £5 a week (£329 in 2019) having to buy their own at prices ranging from £6.14s to £10.18s.

Andersons were cheap and easy to produce. They consisted of corrugated steel sections with a curved roof bolted to sturdy rails to give the structure strength. Ideally, the shelter was then 'planted' three feet into the ground, the remaining exposed sides top-covered with compacted earth at least eighteen inches thick.

Corrugated iron sheets for use as Anderson shelters are pressed into the correct shape at John Summers & Sons, Shotton Steelworks. 13 February 1939. (Marsh. *Liverpool Echo*).

There were instances of people without access to a garden erecting their Anderson inside their homes - but without the protection offered by sandbags piled over and around. They would have been of little use save as a refuge from shards of glass and the like.

Providing the instructions were adhered to, Andersons were surprisingly robust. In a series of load-bearing tests at Shotton Steel Works, pig iron ingots were stacked on top of an Anderson to get the structure to buckle. Engineers managed to balance 75 tons worth of ingots on top with no effect whatsoever. During the Blitz, it was found that Andersons would survive almost anything save a direct hit from a bomb. Depending upon ground conditions, it was found that during the winter months Andersons could become waterlogged. This made their use more than a little unpleasant and during raids some households preferred to take their chance staying in their homes rather than being up to their knees in muddy water. Even so, at least 3 million Andersons were built.

Morrison Shelters

The Morrison shelter was designed specifically for use in the home by those who had neither a garden nor a backyard. Named after Home Secretary and Minister of Home Security Herbert Morrison, this new type of shelter looked like a table. IKEA was founded in Sweden in July 1943, however, the flatpack table, albeit an air-raid shelter, became available to UK households in February 1941.

The carcass measuring 6 ft 6 ins (length) x 4 ft (width) x 2 ft 6 ins (height) or 1970 mm x 1270 mm x 745 mm, was steel fitted with wire mesh sides. It could be assembled by two people in a couple of hours and had to be installed on the lowest floor of the house. There was enough room for two adults and, depending on their size,

In August 1939, residents of Links Avenue, Monkseaton, banded together to construct their own communal air raid shelter. (*Newcastle Chronicle & Journal*).

one or two children. And yes, many used them as kitchen tables.

Once again, they proved robust with occupants surviving the collapse of two and three storey houses. By the end of the war at least one million Morrisons had been issued.

Hudson Shelters

Dating from early 1939, the Hudson was manufactured from Dalzo rust-resisting plates and weighed about 13 cwt (660.4 kg). It was designed to hold up to four people and, when properly sandbagged, would give protection against splinters, the blast from high explosive bombs and overhead cover from incendiaries. The Hudson was cylindrical and tall enough for people to stand in it upright. The plating was rivetted. Manufactured by Thomas Hudson Ltd, Coatbridge, early examples were offered for sale at £30 (£1975.66p in 2019) each.

ARP

On 1 September 1939, instructions were issued to local authorities to put the air raid warning system into full operation. The use of factory hooters and sirens was prohibited except for giving an air raid warning which was done by a series of short blasts. The 'raiders passed' or 'all clear' signal on a factory siren would be a continuous blast lasting two minutes.

Evening newspapers published further information in their Late News columns. All part-time members of the Auxiliary Fire Service were to report to their stations. Many papers carried a police ARP notice to the public. 'Precautions must be taken immediately by all concerned.' No light from a house, office, factory or anywhere else for that matter was to be observable from outside. Dark curtains must be used wherever possible. All illuminated advertising signs and external lights of all kinds must be extinguished except

Boys from Yardley Primary School lend a hand filling sandbags. 1 September 1939. (*Birmingham Post & Mail*).

for any specially authorised traffic or railway signal lights or other specially exempted lights. Lights on vehicles on roads must also be dimmed and screened. The police would issue a leaflet explaining the restrictions to anyone who wanted one.

Yet, on 17 September, the *Sunday Chronicle* carried a report that accusations had been made during a meeting of Hythe (Kent) Council that ARP wardens were not only paid too much but they had nothing to do all day except play darts, drink tea, and smoke. ARP headquarters hit back, denying the allegations. One warden pointed out that only around twenty per cent of people were paid the maximum of £3 a week. The following week, the Government used the lack of air raids as an opportunity to scale back ARP and a review was ordered to find ways of scaling back manpower and costs.

As usual, the government was after something for nothing. The aim was to save money without reducing efficiency.

A conference between Sir John Anderson, Secretary of State for Home Affairs, and local authorities was to be called to thrash out ARP. Up for consideration was maintaining ARP strength in large cities and at the ports as well as the round-the-clock staffing of ARP report centres, but handing over street patrols to volunteers. Also, that a large proportion of ARP duties in small towns and rural areas could be undertaken by volunteers.

The role of the AFS was also to be scrutinised. One idea was to maintain a nucleus of trained personnel supplemented by volunteers as and when required. The Government wanted employers to allow workers to enrol as volunteers for ARP and AFS duties. For example, at the beginning of the war, the Government schedule for Nottingham allowed the city to have 8970 ARP workers. The city's actual strength stood at 8796 of which 2738 were being paid. The city laid-off 349 full-timers to save £50,000 (£3,292,774 in 2019).

The *Newcastle Chronicle's* decontamination squad. (*Newcastle Chronicle & Journal*).

Mrs Picton, Science mistress at Surbiton High School, and part-time warden. (Bernard Alfieri, *Mirrorpix*).

The day war broke out. With the blackout regulations coming into force at sunset, workmen paint white squares on curb stones along the main Birmingham to Coventry road. (*Birmingham Post & Mail*).

To be seen in the blackout, Mr A K Fincham of the Robin Hood Inn, Alfreton, Derbyshire, used four white painted metal pub trays fixed one to each corner front and back. The regulations also required drivers to paint vehicle running boards and wing tips white. (*Derby Telegraph*).

Fitting blackout shields. (*Mirrorpix*).

(Above). The lights start going out as the blackout comes into force in Coventry. Between September 1939 and the end of the year, there were 4000 blackout related deaths in the UK. During the same period, the British Expeditionary Force did not suffer its first casualty until 9 December, when a soldier of the King's Shropshire Light Infantry was killed by friendly fire after triggering a booby trap. (*Coventry Evening Telegraph*).

(Left). A model sports the very latest in blackout fashion accessories – white armlets and waist bands. The Men's Wear Council also recommended men to wear light coloured clothes. The Daily Mirror persuaded several ladies to try the armbands. One said. "People stared at me through the dark, so I knew at once they could be seen and that the experiment was successful. When I crossed the road at pedestrian crossings oncoming cars pulled up at once. The night before, when I wasn't wearing the bands, I had to jump out of the way every time I crossed the road." (*Daily Mirror*).

Mothers collect respirator helmets for their babies from the Carnegie Institute, Hunters Road, Hockley. September 1939. (*Birmingham Post & Mail*).

Gas mask distribution in Birmingham. 1939. (*Birmingham Post & Mail*).

Bedworth ARP hold a training exercise. (*Coventry Evening Telegraph*).

A gas-proof kennel displayed by the animal charity the PDSA. Gasmasks were provided for horses. (*Daily Mirror*).

Boys of St Chad's Roman Catholic School at Birmingham Snow Hill station on 26 August 1939. Birmingham was one of the authorities that held an exercise as early as 20 July 1939, when the pupils and staff from nine schools were taken to Hockley, the first station out of Snow Hill on the GWR main line to Wolverhampton. (*Birmingham Post & Mail*).

The exodus under way from Birmingham Moor Street station on 1 September 1939. As with many other towns and cities, the lack of bombing resulted in the gradual drift back home. The was a second evacuation for some following the raid during the night of 25/26 April 1940, and a further evacuation following the raid of 22/23 November, when a direct hit on Bristol Road South severed the water supply to part of the city. (*Birmingham Post & Mail*).

Children from All Saint's School, Gateshead, arriving at Gateshead station for evacuation. 1 September 1939. (*Newcastle Chronicle & Journal*).

(Page opposite). Accompanied by some of their teachers, children from the Sacred Heart School, Liverpool, make their way to Edge Hill railway station. (*Liverpool Echo*).

Operation Pied Piper

During the early months of 1939, parents up and down the country received a letter from their local education authority advising them that they were in an area deemed at risk from bombing in the event of war, and that plans were being drawn up to evacuate children to places of safety though no indication was given as to where the places of safety where.

"Under the arrangements which are being made the children would gather at the primary school nearest their homes and the older and younger members of each family would as far as possible be evacuated together. They would go to the chosen places in the care of teachers who would remain with them. They would live in the country in houses where they would be welcome. Arrangements would be made to let you know their new addresses as quickly as possible. Children under school age would also be allowed to go if the mother or a woman friend went with them, and all the children of one family would be sent to the same place."

During July 1939, evacuation theory was put into practice when schools in several cities took part in rehearsals. To test the procedure for getting people from their designated assembly points to their point of departure, pupils and staff from nine schools in Birmingham descended upon Hockley, the first station out of Snow Hill on the GWR main line to Wolverhampton.

As the international situation deteriorated during late summer, some schools took matters into their own hands and relocated. St Chad's Roman Catholic Boys School left Birmingham by train on Saturday 26 August, the day all schools in evacuation areas in England and Scotland had been ordered to reopen to prepare for a nationwide rehearsal the following Monday. Meetings were held at every school to advise parents and children of what to expect during the rehearsals.

Though the Monday was only a rehearsal, plans were in place that, should it prove necessary, the exercise could quickly be turned into the real evacuation. All school children who were at home were to be at their appropriate assembly school by 9.00am. Mothers with children under the age of five were also invited to take part.

Each child should, if possible, bring with them the articles required should the actual evacuation take place. A warm coat or mackintosh, night clothes, a change of underwear and a change of stockings or socks, house shoes or rubber shoes, toothbrush, comb, towel, bar of soap and a face cloth. They should also bring enough food for the day, a tin cup, plate, and their gasmask in its box.

Each child was to wear an identity label listing the child's name, date of birth, home address, name of school attended and destination. There was to be one adult, usually a teacher, for every ten children. Adults travelling on the trains would wear a white armband, usually sporting the initials of the relevant education authority. Should the rehearsal become the real thing, teachers fortunate enough to own cars would go by road to their allotted reception areas. The reasoning behind this was that a school might well be dispersed in groups across several villages, and the cars would come in handy, keeping the groups in contact with one another.

There were exceptions to the rehearsal schedules. Because of the proximity of the naval base, Rosyth was the only part of the burgh of Dunfermline scheduled for evacuation. However, its local schools, King's Road, Park Road, and the Roman Catholic School, decided to hold normal lessons on the morning of the 28th and their evacuation rehearsal during the afternoon. Like other schools in the designated evacuation areas, they were open the previous weekend so that teachers could issue instructions and answer parents' questions and queries.

The Press listed the designated evacuation areas as London; Tottenham, East Ham, Acton, Willesden, West Ham, Walthamstow, Stratford, Leyton, Edmonton, Barking, Ilford, Rochester, Southampton, Chatham, and Gosport. In the midlands and the north west; Coventry, Birmingham, Smethwick, Derby, Nottingham, Liverpool, Bootle, Crosby, Birkenhead, Wallasey, Manchester, and Salford. In the north;

Hull, Grimsby, Bradford, Leeds, Rotherham, and Sheffield. In the north east and Scotland; Newcastle-upon-Tyne, Gateshead, Edinburgh, Glasgow, Clydebank, Dundee, and Rosyth.

"It is very important that there should be a complete muster of children at present in the evacuation areas, but children away from home need not be specially brought back."

On 31 August, special messengers advised schools that the evacuation would commence the next day, Friday 1 September, and continue through the weekend or even longer where required, regardless of the international situation. Some towns such as Grimsby did not receive the final go-ahead until late afternoon, early evening, by which time the shops were closed, leaving parents unable to obtain clothing and other last-minute items.

In Grimsby, the children assembled at their respective schools. The first groups away were from Hilda Street, Weelsby Road and Holme Hill. The *Grimsby Evening Telegraph* reported that Burgh, Mablethorpe, Horncastle, Skegness and Woodall Spa were that day's destinations and that Scunthorpe and other places in north Lincolnshire would be receiving children from Hull. Surprisingly, few parents were at the Hull Corporation Pier to see the children board the paddle steamer *Wingfield Castle* for the trip across the Humber – there was no bridge back then. On arrival at New Holland, the children transferred to buses for their onward journeys.

The number of children evacuated from Hull and Grimsby fell far below expectations. It was a similar story in many other towns and cities such as Birmingham, where fewer than one third of the 73,000 children entitled to be evacuated turned up.

Originally, some places such as Sheffield had put forward their own schemes. In Sheffield's case the local educational authority had proposed sending its evacuees to the neighbouring and familiar area of north Derbyshire. The Government in its infinite wisdom knew better, advising the Sheffield Emergency Committee in April 1939 that 30,200 places had been secured in Leicestershire and a further 30,100 in Nottinghamshire.

At Sheffield, the London & North Eastern Railway laid on twenty special trains to a variety of destinations including Newark, Bingham,

Ruddington, Loughborough and Melton Mowbray. Many of the trains carried only a third of the children expected. The second evacuation train from Sheffield Victoria to Newark had places for 840 children but carried only 266. The response had not been great with only fifteen per cent of those registered leaving. The city attempted a second trawl, schools opening on 11 September for teachers to take names of prospective evacuees. Thirty-five minutes after opening, the Cathedral School had not taken a single name, and Carbrook Council School managed to register only eleven children in the first hour.

In the London boroughs, fewer than half of the 400,000 registered children left. On the other hand, Manchester, where a well-organized evacuation scheme had been put in place, saw 75 per cent of its children leave. Around 170,000 children and mothers were evacuated from the Scottish designated areas to the comparative safety of the country and west coast seaside towns. On Tyneside, 44,000 were evacuated over the first two days of September, though several days later Wallsend and South Shields were among the local areas still evacuating people.

Most parties were within marching distance of a railway station, though at Derby the corporation's entire fleet of petrol buses as well as twenty buses from Trent Motor Traction were pressed into service on the Saturday to take 2200 children to various locations around Clay Cross and Chesterfield. On Sunday, a mixed bag of children from infant, junior, and secondary schools were evacuated from Derby, the majority sent just a few miles south to the Shardlow area, though 1000 ended up around Belper and Ripley. All in all, few of Derby's evacuees were more than fifteen miles from the town.

Evacuees from Birmingham were scattered in all directions. Many of the city's evacuation trains started from New Street, Moor Street or Snow Hill, picking up parties at suburban stations as they went. Some, such as Boulton Road Junior School, Handsworth, travelled the short distance to Hagley, whilst others finished up billeted around villages and farms in Derbyshire, Herefordshire, and Monmouthshire. Wherever Birmingham's children were sent, the Education Department stipulated that no child must be more than three and a half hours travelling time from their homes.

Coventry was a late addition to the list for evacuation. Indeed, the Government had initially designated it as a safe area, and it was only after some serious lobbying from the council that the overcrowded districts were included in evacuation planning. As it was, only 3200 children out of the 8625 registered turned up at their assembly points on 4 September. Additionally, the city evacuated 922 others comprising mothers with children under school age, the disabled and the visually impaired.

As with many other towns and cities, most of Coventry's kids travelled short distances to places such as Wellesbourne and Kenilworth, though the boys of Bablake School went on an awfully big adventure and ended up at Lincoln.

Smiles all round as the guard looks along the length of his train. 2 September 1939. Merseyside's evacuees were spread far and wide. Among them, Cole Street School, Birkenhead, went to Bangor in Wales; Walton Lane Council School, Liverpool, ended up at Aveley, Shropshire; St George's Church School were sent to Harlech, and Holy Trinity School, Anfield, went to Aberystwyth. (*Liverpool Echo*).

It was a similar short distance for the children of the Northern Secondary School, Southampton. They were evacuated in two groups on 1 September. In the morning, 400 girls and 150 boys together with teaching staff and helpers made the twelve-mile (19km) journey to Winchester. That evening, they were joined by a further 300 boys together with helpers and the remaining teachers. Winchester was divided into billeting areas with a master in charge of each one.

Nationwide, between 31 August and 8 September, more than 1.5 million people were evacuated to designated safe areas. The figure comprised 827,000 children, 524,000 mothers and young children, 13,000 expectant mothers, 7000 handicapped people and 103,000 teachers and helpers. Even these figures, impressive as they are and considering that not one serious or fatal accident occurred, was far fewer than the Government had hoped for.

Where the children finished up being billeted was anyone's guess. Though taking in an evacuee was voluntary, billeting officers were given compulsory powers and could force a household to take evacuees. Households were paid 10s 6d (52.2p) a week for each unaccompanied child they took in and 8s 6d (42.2p) a week for each child and

mother. Some slum children finished up in the homes of the wealthy while some children from wealthy families ended up living in slums. One of the better-known stories involved a mother and her young child from a Glasgow tenement. Billeted with a well-to-do family in the countryside, all was going well until the toddler squatted down in the middle of the room to defecate on an expensive Persian carpet. Seeing the look of horror on her host's face, the mother was quick to admonish the child with the words, "Don't do it on the nice lady's carpet. Go and do it in the corner like at home."

The use of toilets was not the only problem. Many of the children were infested with lice. As the evacuation programme had commenced at the start of the new school year, most schools had had insufficient time to organise their annual après summer holidays delousing parades.

At a meeting of the Newcastle and Gateshead Band of Hope Union, Lady Trevelyan stated she was shocked to hear a story concerning an evacuated child in the south of England who, when on arrival at his billet, and asked if he would like some biscuits replied, "Biscuits? What I want is beer and chips. That's what I get at Home."

Evacuees arriving at East Ham station on 3 September. (*Daily Mirror*).

At the other end of the scale were the six boys who found themselves billeted with the retired colonel of the Durham Light Infantry. He lived in a large house by the river at Romaldkirk and the old boy filled their idle hours teaching them the rudiments of infantry training in his extensive grounds. From the reports, it was fun all round for all concerned. However, what was not fun were reports of wealthy and middle class households who, having taken in people under extreme sufferance, then turned their 'guests' out onto the streets so they could entertain friends and family over the Christmas period.

Within a surprisingly short time, the children in the nearer evacuation areas began drifting back to their homes. What started as a trickle soon turned into a flood. As early as 29 September 1939, it is estimated that 800 children had returned to Coventry, even though their schools were closed. It was a similar story elsewhere. By early October, the drift back was noticeable in Sheffield. In one case, two children aged seven and nine set out to walk from Leicestershire and by hitch-hiking managed to arrive back home in Sheffield by the evening of the same day.

As the weeks went by with no bombing, many parents were tempted to have their children back. It is estimated that by the end of March 1940, three quarters of those children evacuated from Glasgow had returned home.

Soon, so many children had returned that schools reopened though it is true that many did this with less than half of their pre-war complement of pupils. The drift back continued throughout the Phoney War. Despite the return of children in large numbers, there remained a steady stream of evacuees leaving London and major industrial centres, many having made private arrangements to stay with relatives. When the Blitz began, it is estimated that at least 500,000 children who were eligible for evacuation were living in the London boroughs.

There would be further evacuations caused by the fall of France, the Blitz, as well as the V1 and V2 attacks.

Evacuees at a London station. 3 September. (*Daily Mirror*).

(Left). Checking the label. Two young Londoners await the next phase of their journey. (*Daily Mirror*).

(Page opposite top). Smiles for the camera from the pupils of the Richardson Dees School, Wallsend, awaiting evacuation to Ponteland. 6 September 1939. (*Newcastle Chronicle & Journal*).

(Page opposite bottom). Mothers with young children make their way to the station at South Shields. (*Newcastle Chronicle & Journal*).

Walworth Central School crosses the Elephant and Castle on the way to their receiving station for evacuation. (Bernard Alfieri. *Daily Mirror*).

(Top). Children, from Glasgow on their way to Glengonnar at Abington, South Lanarkshire. It was one of five outdoor residential education centres constructed in Scotland during late 1939, early 1940. The others were Belmont Centre at Meigle, Broomlee at West Linton, Dounans Outdoor Camp at Aberfoyle, and Middleton at Gorebridge. Similar centres were also built in England and Wales.

The camps were a Department of Health initiative, the intention being to give children from inner cities the opportunity to enjoy clean air and a healthy diet. Each of the camps could accommodate around 250 children plus teachers and camp-site staff. With the outbreak of war, it was decided to use the camps for evacuees.
(*Daily Record*).

(Page opposite top). Evacuees from Heaton, Newcastle upon Tyne, "somewhere in Northumberland" on 17 September 1939. (*Newcastle Chronicle & Journal*).

(Page opposite bottom). Somewhere in deepest Derbyshire, a school woodwork room has been pressed into service as a classroom for a group of children evacuated from the Manchester area. 15 September 1939. (*Derby Telegraph*).

(Right). Mrs Rixon, wife of the headmaster of St Michael's School, Buckingham Palace Road, Pimlico, makes sure pupils have all their belongings, prior to the school evacuating. (*Daily Mirror*).

Fashions for the home front? The very latest from a shop in Birmingham. From left to right: a bib and brace with sweater ensemble; a bed quilt come wrap, and a pair of 1939 onesies. (*Birmingham Post & Mail*).

A 'freshly planted' Anderson shelter 4 September 1939. There were instances where people completely missed the point, erecting their Andersons indoors without adding additional protection such as sandbags. (*Newcastle Chronical & Journal*).

The Home Front

Sunday 3 September 1939 saw a flurry of emergency regulations and precautionary measures put in place. As well as the immediate closure of all places of entertainment and sports fixtures likely to attract large crowds, people were expected to keep off the streets unless it was necessary for them to be out.

The Board of Trade immediately banned the import of all goods that could be supplied by UK-based manufacturers. The first list, released on 4 September, included, pottery and glassware, cutlery, textiles, clothing, footwear, clocks and watches, toiletries, perfume, makeup, luxury foodstuffs, toys and games, musical instruments, motorcars, certain listed chemicals, paints, and office equipment.

Also announced was the rationing of petrol from 16 September. Petroleum distributors were to pool all supplies and only one grade would be supplied to the public. It was to be called 'Pool' motor spirit and sold at the fixed price of 1. 6d (7.5p) a gallon (4.54 litres). The ex-pump price of 'Pool' was fixed for at least fourteen days, and garages were free to sell off their remaining stocks of individual brands of petrol. An announcement would be made on 4 September as to applying for petrol ration books.

Anyone owning gold coins or foreign exchange was required to take it to the bank and sell it to the Treasury. Currencies already listed included: US dollars, French francs, Swiss francs, Guilders, Swedish crowns, and Argentinian pesos. Businesses requiring gold and foreign exchange to meet contracts made before the declaration of war had to apply through their bankers. It was now illegal to export gold, banknotes, or foreign currency. Later in the war, the actor Noel Coward was convicted of racketeering and fined £1600 (£81,378 in 2019) for failing to register his US dollars with the Treasury.

It was the Americans who first coined the phrase 'Phoney War' for the period from 3 September up to the German invasion of Norway in April 1940. But at sea there was nothing phoney at all about the war. Within hours of the declaration, the Donaldson Line passenger ship SS *Athenia* en route to Montreal was torpedoed without warning and sunk. Within 48 hours the destroyers HMS *Electra* and HMS *Escort* were unceremoniously dumping the survivors at Greenock. No provision had been made to deal with them and, as confusion reigned as to who was to pay for what, a large drapery store in the town supplied clothing and footwear for men, women and children, and a local car hire firm organised hot tea, buns, sandwiches and other food. Many survivors had no money and initially the Donaldson Line refused to provide funds for onward transportation. By the end of September, nearly all Athenia's survivors had managed to get away, the Donaldson Line contributing £5325 (£350,680 in 2019) towards the costs.

The *Athenia* incident also gave the country its first spy scare. An American by the name of Gustav Anderson, who was already known to have smuggled photographs out of the USSR, had recently returned from Europe. When *Athenia* called at Liverpool on 2 September, Anderson photographed the balloon barrage through a porthole whilst the other passengers were in the dining room. It was also alleged he was pro-Nazi in his political views. As a neutral, the British authorities were unable to take him into custody for questioning.

By the end of September, forty merchant ships and fishing vessels had been sunk by U-boats, nine had been mined, and one, the SS *Clement*, had been sunk by a surface raider. In all, 189,000 tons of shipping had been sent to the bottom. By the end of the year, losses amounted to 760,000 tons. The U-boats had claimed 103 victims, a further 83 had been mined, fifteen had been sunk by surface raiders, and the Luftwaffe had accounted for ten others.

The RAF's first taste of action came on the morning of 6 September, when at 6.15am radar picked up unidentified aircraft approaching the Essex coast at high altitude from the east. The Hurricanes of 56 Squadron were scrambled from North Weald as well as the Hornchurch-based Spitfires of 54, 65 and 74 Squadrons. For good measure, the Hurricanes of North Weald's 151 Squadron also took to the air.

Unfortunately, none of the pilots had seen action and only one or two are thought to have ever seen a German fighter or bomber. And so, during what later became known as the Battle of Barking Creek, several Spitfires from 74 Squadron opened fire on several Hurricanes from 56 Squadron. Pilot Officer Montague Hutton-Harrop of 56 Squadron became the first RAF pilot to be killed since the commencement of hostilities. His Hurricane was the first aircraft to be shot down by a Spitfire. His colleague, Pilot Officer Frank Rose, became the first pilot of the war to survive a forced landing. Shaken, but otherwise unharmed, he brought his shot-up Hurricane to earth at Whersted, between Ipswich and Manningtree.

Further south, the aircraft of 65 Squadron were fired on by a number of our anti-aircraft batteries because the gunners could not read Morse code, thus failing to recognize the significance of the messages the pilots were sending on their aircraft's downward identification lights. And the radar warning? That was a false alarm.

On 7 September, just four days after the declaration of war, petrol ration books were issued for the first time and by the beginning of November the Government was warning garages that forged petrol coupons were already

Survivors from the *Athenia* in Glasgow. 5 September 1939. (*Daily Record*).

in circulation. Of course, there were ways of circumventing petrol rationing. One, simply drive off without paying, and two, steal the stuff from the armed forces. This latter activity was proving so popular that by May 1940 military fuel was dyed and the police were mounting random checks on the contents of civilian petrol tanks.

The Fuel & Lighting Order also came into effect on 7 September, its aim to reduce the total quarterly consumption of electricity to 75 per cent of the amount used in the quarter ending 30 June 1939. Twelve days later it was announced that coal rationing would start on 1 October. Householders were required to register with a licensed coal merchant and would then be advised by a local official as to their basic quantity entitlement each quarter.

In January 1940, sugar, bacon, and butter went on ration. However, as many working-class families could not afford butter and could rarely afford streaky bacon, which according to the J Sainsbury archive were 1s 3d (6.5p) and 1s 6d (7.5p) per pound respectively, stockpiles soon built up and

the Government decreed double rations at no additional cost for everyone. For those unable to afford butter, margarine made from whale oil with added vitamins was available at 6d (2.5p) per pound.

The weekly ration allowance per person was two ounces (56.7 grams) of tea (none for the under-fives), two ounces each of butter, sweets, and fats, four ounces (113 grams) each of margarine and sugar. Extra cheese was issued to workers with no canteen facilities and a special ration was organised for vegetarians, though they were forced to surrender their meat coupons. Prime cuts of meat were rationed at six ounces (170 grams) per person per day, though people were free to buy quantities of cheaper cuts up to the cash value of six ounces of prime beef, mutton, or pork.

Under the Defence Regulations, it was illegal for shopkeepers to sell rationed goods without coupons. Shopkeepers were deliberately targeted by the Food Office which sent undercover operatives into shops with the sole intention of persuading the shopkeeper to part with a rationed

A Morrison shelter in use as a table. In fact, some early government publicity refers to them as Table Shelters. (Official. *Mirrorpix*).

item without receiving the appropriate coupon in exchange. The operatives were at liberty to try any hard luck story they cared to come up with and to persevere until the shopkeeper either handed over the goods or refused point blank. Any shopkeeper falling for the hard luck story was then prosecuted under the regulations. As it was a strict liability offence, the shopkeeper was guilty as charged.

Shopkeepers and traders took the used coupons they had collected to the Post Office where they were exchanged for a voucher. The voucher, could then be set against their next wholesale purchase. The regulations required that the used coupons be returned to the appropriate issuing office where they would be checked. This soon proved totally unworkable. Millions and millions of coupons were soon sloshing around the country and whatever the security was, it was not fit for purpose. The Ministry of Food kept up the pretence that every coupon was checked whereas, in reality, it was very small percentage indeed. It did not take long for the underworld and unscrupulous shopkeepers to catch on that there was no way the ministry could check every coupon. The Post Office, responsible for collection and shipment of coupons, had been overwhelmed in a matter of days and immediately modified the system so it could cope by refusing to check or count coupons handed in. Shopkeepers and traders

could take in their bundles of coupons which they simply signed for. The unscrupulous shopkeeper got his all-important voucher and, in return, the ministry got a bundle of coupon-sized newspaper clippings or blank paper bearing a bogus name and address.

Other targets for the Food Office were cafes and restaurants. Under the regulations, it was a strict liability offence to serve a customer more than two-courses, though it was not illegal for a customer to pay for their two-course meal, leave the restaurant, then come back in, sit at a different table and order two more, possibly different courses. The meal-snooper's task was to persuade staff into serving them a larger meal than permitted. Not only was the restaurant automatically guilty, so too was the poor waiter or waitress who were charged with 'aiding and abetting.' The British Restaurants established during the war appear not to have attracted too much attention from the Food Office as they had set menus, guaranteeing the customer a decent meal for a set price.

Inspectors were also given powers to enter homes and check the contents of the larder. Before the war, housewives who kept a well-stocked larder were applauded. Now they were hoarders. Mrs Elsie Carter, of Caversham was fined £36. 15s

(£2072. 74p in 2019) for hoarding. Mind you, the contents of Elsie's larder were a little on the excessive side - 75 pounds (34.02 kg) of preserves; 98 tins of mixed fruit; 82 tins of milk; 81 tins of meat, and 196 tins of fish.

When Sir John Simon announced the Budget to the Commons in April 1940, he spoke for two hours and seven minutes. During that time, he revealed the estimated expenditure for the coming year was £2,667,000,000 (£150,421,440,650 in 2019) of which £1,234,000,000 (£42,602,915,186 in 2019) would come from revenue. Income tax was raised from 7s to 7s 6d in the pound and surtax was to be levied on those earning more than £1500 (£84,601 in 2019) a year. Beer went up by 1d a pint, whiskey by 1s 9d (9p) a bottle to 16s (80p), and there were increases on tobacco duty, postal charges, and telephone calls.

1940 also saw the introduction of a points system of rationing on clothing and tinned meats. Tinned crab, salmon, oranges, pineapple, lemons and so on were not officially rationed because they were almost impossible to get hold of.

In December 1941, a second National Service Act was passed. Unmarried women aged 20-30 and childless widows became liable for conscription mainly due to not enough of them volunteering for the women's sections of the armed forces. Men up to the age of 60 became liable for some form of National Service including military for those up to the age of 51.

In February 1942, Sir Stafford Cripps told the Commons that "personal extravagance must be eliminated altogether." No petrol for pleasure motoring, a cut in the clothing ration and sporting events curtailed. Cigarettes were not officially rationed though many tobacconists looked after their regular customers first. Silk stockings became a thing of the past and women resorted to painting their legs with gravy browning. In 1938, more than 33 million pairs of stockings were imported - but by 1944 it had dropped to 718,000 pairs, not including those that might be had from American bases.

The clothing ration in 1945 was 48 coupons. A man's suit of utility cloth took 24 coupons and soldiers being discharged early on medical grounds could make a small fortune selling their demob suit. The outfit on Civvy Street would have cost around £12 (£522 in 2019) and included a shirt, two collars, a tie, two pairs of socks, a pair of shoes, a raincoat, and a felt hat. The army valued the whole lot at £11 (£478 in 2019) though the price could be upped as the buyer stood to save 56 coupons.

The images on these two pages were taken during an ARP exercise at Derby in 1939. (Page opposite) The RAF detachment mounting guard at the LNER station at Friargate. (Above). Workers take cover at Qualcast Ltd, Victory Road. (*Derby Telegraph*).

In May 1935, Parliament passed the Military Training Act, requiring single men aged 20-22 to undertake six months military training. About 240,000 signed up.

Militiamen training on Bren light machine guns mounted on anti-aircraft tripods at the South Staffordshire Regimental Depot. September 1939. (*Birmingham Post & Mail*).

A scene that must have been repeated countless times across the UK during September 1939 as local Territorial Army units set off for France. Here the 8th (Ardwick) Battalion, Manchester Regiment, bring traffic to a standstill as they march through the city centre. At the time, the battalion formed the 127th Infantry Brigade along with the 5th Manchesters and the 4th East Lancs and were a part of the 42nd (East Lancashire) Infantry Division commanded by Major-General W G Holmes.

The Division's home headquarters were in Manchester. Other units raised around Manchester included the 52nd (Manchester) Regiment Royal Artillery, and the 42nd Royal Tank Regiment.

Manchester units were also serving with the 66th Infantry Division, including the 6th and 7th Manchesters, which with the 2/8thh Lancashire Fusiliers comprised the 199th Infantry Brigade. Three locally raised Royal Engineer units, the 255th, 256th and 258th Field Park Companies, were also assigned to the 66th. (*Manchester Evening News*).

From 27 December 1939 to 18 February 1940, the UK suffered its most severe winter since 1895, with frost, heavy snow and ice bringing road, rail, canal, and air traffic to a halt. The Grand Union Canal between Birmingham and London was frozen throughout. The port of Southampton was iced over. While Britain experienced temperatures as low as -8C, it was even colder in Europe where the temperature dropped to between -20C and -28C. (Above). The river tug *Thames* making its way along the frozen river Thames at Teddington. (Below). One way of delivering milk in the freezing conditions. (*Mirrorpix*).

YOUR NEW 'RATION' BOOK

HOW TO REGISTER WITH THE SHOPS

The new Ration Books are now being distributed. As soon as you receive your new Book you must fill in the particulars as explained below, and then take the Book to the shops for fresh Registration. It has been found possible to allow *immediate* Registration, and the sooner you register the better.

Weighing meat at Derby Wholesale Market prior to its distribution to butchers under Government regulations. January 1940. (*Derby Telegraph*).

(Page opposite top left). Photograph of a grocer's window in Bristol shortly after the introduction of rationing on 8 January 1940 on bacon, butter, and sugar. Margarine is on offer at 8d (3.5p) per lb, whereas the Sainsbury archives give the price of butter at the time as 1s 3d (7.5p) per lb. Half a dozen eggs for 10d (5p) is on the expensive side given they were usually 1s 3d a dozen. (*Bristol Post*).

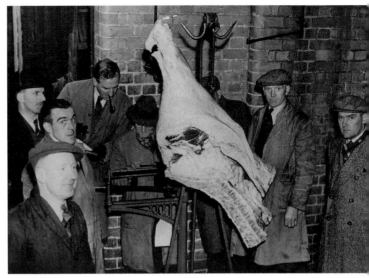

Shoppers in Derby Market Hall check out the recipes and hints on nutrition at the on the Kitchen Front exhibition organized by Derby Education Committee. 1940. Housewives would soon be bombarded with recipes and useful hints. (*Derby Telegraph*).

Collecting the coal ration. Households were rationed to 2.5 tons (2267.96kg) a year. Today, this appears to be generous but back then houses often had coal-fired water boilers separate from kitchen ranges. It was always the norm to have only one room heated with a coal fire unless someone was ill when a bedroom grate might be lit. (*Birmingham Post & Mail*).

(Page opposite bottom). Ration books are prepared for distribution at the Derby Food Office. Ration books had a black-market value of £5 each (£282 in 2019), ration books were a prime target for burglars. The biggest haul being the 100,000 unused and unmarked books taken from the Food Office at Romford. (*Derby Telegraph*)

The Phoney War is over, and Britain looks to home defence. On Monday, 13 May, the *Daily Mirror* reported that many roads had barricades guarded by armed sentries. It was the same day that Churchill gave his first speech as Prime Minister. The war would be a slogging match. In the end we would be victorious but in the meantime all Churchill could offer was, "blood, toil, tears and sweat."

This image was published on page 9 of the following day's edition, the report indicating that roadblocks had been established in coastal areas mainly to guard against, "fifth columnist 'Quislings' and enemy parachutists." All motorists stopped at one of these roadblocks had to show their identification cards. (*Mirrorpix*).

Due to the imminent threat of invasion, children from south coast (Kent and Sussex) towns were evacuated further inland. An evacuation train at Belper, Derbyshire, on 15 June 1940. (*Derby Telegraph*).

(Page opposite top). Nuns on the run. The roundup of aliens was under way in Derby on 28 May 1940. These ladies are on their way to internment on the Isle of Man. (*Derby Telegraph*).

(Page opposite bottom). Alien internees are marched through Liverpool to the docks from where they will be taken by ship to the Isle of Man. Lord Beaverbrook moved quickly to have Jewish German engineers released so they could work on Ministry of Aircraft Production projects. (*Mirrorpix*).

RATIONING
of Clothing, Cloth, Footwear
from June 1, 1941

Rationing has been introduced, not to deprive you of your real needs, but to make more certain that you get your share of the country's goods—to get fair shares with everybody else.

When the shops re-open you will be able to buy cloth, clothes, footwear and knitting wool *only if you bring your Food Ration Book with you.* The shopkeeper will detach the required number of coupons from the unused margarine page. Each margarine coupon counts as one coupon towards the purchase of clothing or footwear. You will have a total of 66 coupons to last you for a year; so go sparingly. You can buy *where* you like and *when* you like without registering.

NUMBER OF COUPONS NEEDED

Men and Boys	Adult	Child	Women and Girls	Adult	Child
Unlined mackintosh or cape	9	7	Lined mackintoshes, or coats (over 28 in. in length)	14	11
Other mackintoshes, or raincoat, or overcoat	16	11	Jacket, or short coat (under 28 in. in length)	11	8
Coat, or jacket, or blazer or like garment	13	8	Dress, or gown, or frock—woollen	11	8
Waistcoat, or pull-over, or cardigan, or jersey	5	3	Dress, or gown, or frock—other material	7	5
Trousers (other than fustian or corduroy)	8	6	Gym tunic, or girl's skirt with bodice	8	6
Fustian or corduroy trousers	5	5	Blouse, or sports shirt, or cardigan, or jumper	5	3
Shorts	5	3	Skirt, or divided skirt	7	5
Overalls, or dungarees or like garment	6	4	Overalls, or dungarees or like garment	6	4
Dressing-gown or bathing-gown	8	6	Apron, or pinafore	3	2
Night-shirt or pair of pyjamas	8	6	Pyjamas	8	6
Shirt, or combinations—woollen	8	6	Nightdress	6	5
Shirt, or combinations—other material	5	4	Petticoat, or slip, or combination, or cami-knickers	4	3
Pants, or vest, or bathing costume, or child's blouse	4	2	Other undergarments, including corsets	3	2
Pair of socks or stockings	3	1	Pair of stockings	2	1
Collar, or tie, or pair of cuffs	1	1	Pair of socks (ankle length)	1	1
Two handkerchiefs	1	1	Collar, or tie, or pair of cuffs	1	1
Scarf, or pair of gloves or mittens	2	2	Two handkerchiefs	1	1
Pair of slippers or goloshes	4	2	Scarf, or pair of gloves or mittens or muff	2	2
Pair of boots or shoes	7	3	Pair of slippers, boots or shoes	5	3
Pair of leggings, gaiters or spats	3	2			

CLOTH. Coupons needed per yard depend on the width. For example, a yard of woollen cloth 16 inches wide requires 3 coupons. The same amount of cotton or other cloth needs 2 coupons.
KNITTING WOOL. 1 coupon for two ounces.

THESE GOODS MAY BE BOUGHT *WITHOUT* COUPONS

¶ Children's clothing of sizes generally suitable for infants less than 4 years old. ¶ Boiler suits and workmen's bib and brace overalls ¶ Hats and caps. ¶ Sewing thread. ¶ Mending wool and mending silk. ¶ Boot and shoe laces. ¶ Tapes, braids, ribbons and other fabrics of 3 inches or less in width. ¶ Elastic. ¶ Lace and lace net. ¶ Sanitary towels. ¶ Braces, suspenders and garters. ¶ Hard haberdashery. ¶ Clogs. ¶ Black-out cloth dyed black. ¶ All second-hand articles.

Special Notice to Retailers

Retailers will be allowed to get fresh stocks of cloth up to and including June 28th, of other rationed goods up to and including June 21st, WITHOUT SURRENDERING COUPONS. After those dates they will be able to obtain fresh stocks only by turning in their customers' coupons. Steps have been taken, in the interests of the smaller retailers, to limit during these periods the quantity of goods which can be supplied by a wholesaler or manufacturer to any one retailer however large his orders. *Further information can be obtained from your Trade Organisations.*

ISSUED BY THE BOARD OF TRADE

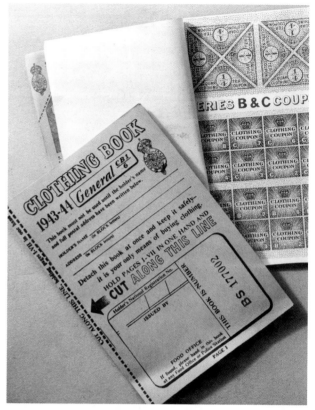

The Women's Voluntary Service ran garment exchanges for children's clothes. When clothes rationing started, people were able to buy cloth, clothes, footwear and knitting wool using coupons from a surplus page of margarine coupons, each counted as one coupon toward the purchase of clothing or footwear. Clothing for children under the age of four was exempt as was wool and silk thread for mending, sewing thread, and boot and shoelaces. (*Daily Mirror*).

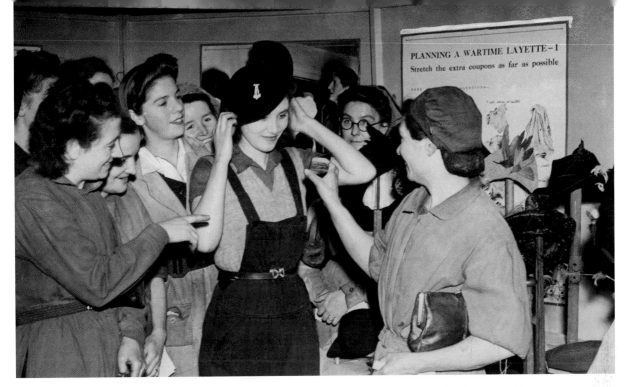

War workers at a London factory organized a make do and mend centre. Miss Lillian Burry tries on a remodelled hat. October 1943. (*Mirrorpix*).

Dress designers pulled out the stops with their Spring 1944 styles. Colours ranged from attractive pastels, through lime green to shades of dusky pink and turquoise blue. With materials being somewhat problematic, most designers used a rayon mixture said to be like a fine wool and warm enough to withstand sudden spring winds. The fashion parade was held in London on Monday, 28 February, 1944. A different image of this dress was published in the following day's edition of the *Daily Mirror*. It was described as an oatmeal crepe dress in hyacinth blue with brown side panels let into the bodice. The pleats of the skirt unpressed. Its Utility value was 53s 7d (approx. £123.06 in 2019). All-day dresses started at 45s 9d (approx. £105.07 in 2019. (Official. *Mirrorpix*).

The ladies of the Heaton Social Service knitting party meet over tea and buns to knit scarves, gloves, socks, and anything else that our troops overseas might need. Taken at Park View House, Heaton, Newcastle. (*Newcastle Chronicle & Journal*).

It is a freezing January 1940 and Derby Corporation Tramways Department is recruiting bus conductresses. Modelling the new uniform is Joan. Joan worked in the tramway offices but when the photographer from the *Evening Telegraph* turned up, she was the only lady around who fitted into it.

In April 1940, a ruling handed down by the Industrial Court awarded corporation bus conductresses equal pay for the war period. For the first six months service, they were to receive 90 per cent of the men's rate of pay, and thereafter the full rate. The women would accept the men's conditions except the guaranteed week might be for 40 hours instead of 48. All work in excess of 40 hours was to be paid at the male overtime rate. (*Derby Telegraph*).

Keeping the wheels turning in Devonshire. Recruits learn the dark arts of the ticket machine. November 1940. (*Torquay Herald Express*).

(Below). It was during Manchester's rush hour, shortly before 8.30am on 12 November 1940, that many of the city's trams and trolley buses started grinding to a halt. Businesses, shops, and houses were without electricity. Scores of shops were forced to work by candlelight; grocers were unable to slice bacon or grind coffee; the lifts in the big stores were at a standstill. Rumours were rife it was the work of Fifth Columnists. However, within thirty minutes, a skeleton bus service was in operation on all routes. As the *Manchester Evening News* later pointed out, the incident was caused by a power failure and not by enemy action. (*Manchester Evening News*).

Day nursery provision became all too important as the war continued, and more and more women went to work to aid the war effort. The Ministry of Health funded the buildings and the local authorities contributed towards running costs. Nursery nurses played a vital role in the welfare of youngsters. (Above). Wash time. (*Mirrorpix*). (At left). Always carry your gasmask. (*Derby Telegraph*). (Below). Not quite a chain gang. Children from Norwich Street Nursery, Cambridge, are out for a stroll, the rope no doubt intended to stop them breaking ranks and scattering. (*Daily Mirror*).

US troops treat youngsters to an afternoon at the movies (*Mirrorpix*). (Below). This image taken at a school in Cardiff, carries a file date of Tuesday, 29 March 1944, the day before St David's Day. (*Mirrorpix*).

DAILY MIRROR, Thursday, April 4, 1940.

Daily Mirror

APL 4

No. 11,332
Registered at the G.P.O. as a Newspaper

ONE PENNY

CHURCHILL WAR LEADER IN NEW CABINET

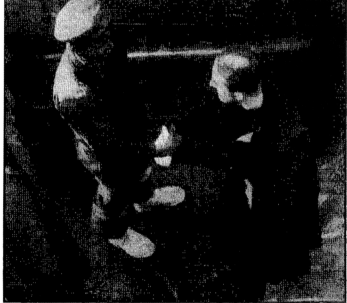

Man with bandaged hand is a German wing commander. He's shaking hands with the skipper of a drifter which shot down his plane and then rescued the crew. OTHER PICTURES ON BACK PAGE.

MR. WINSTON CHURCHILL is from today Britain's War Chief, the number one man of all our fighting forces.

As Mr. Chamberlain announced his Cabinet changes last night he revealed that Lord Chatfield, Defence Minister, has resigned; that his office is abolished and that Mr. Churchill will preside over the regular meetings of the Service Ministers.

These meetings, attended by the Ministers and their chiefs of staff, with Mr. Burgin, Minister of Supply, will deal with all problems of the war and make direct recommendations to the War Cabinet.

And Churchill, in the key position, becomes in fact a wartime Deputy Premier.

In the Cabinet changes Sir Samuel Hoare, Lord Privy Seal, aged sixty, becomes the new Air Minister in place of Sir Kingsley Wood, who takes Sir Samuel's old job

The Food Boss

There is one big surprise. Lord Woolton, better known as Sir Frederick Marquis, chief of Lewis's, Ltd., becomes Food Minister.

Mr. W. S. Morrison, the former Minister of Food, goes to the comparatively unimportant job of Postmaster-General.

Other appointments are:
Mr. R. S. Hudson: Minister of Shipping.
Mr. H. Ramsbotham: Board of Education.
Earl De La Warr: First Commissioner of Works.
Major Tryon: Chancellor of the Duchy of Lancaster.
Mr. Shakespeare: Secretary, Overseas Trade.
Sir Victor Warrender: Financial Secretary, Admiralty.
Sir Edward Grigg: Financial Secretary, War Office.

These changes are largely a reshuffle. Mr. Hudson takes on the job left open by the death of Sir John Gilmour, and Earl De La Warr accepts an unimportant post to make way for Mr. Ramsbotham at the Board of Education.

Mr. Chamberlain, writes the Daily Mirror Political Correspondent, has made his changes determined that there shall be no more complaints that the War Council is out of touch with Home and Service difficulties.

Complete co-ordination has been his aim.

The new appointments have been submitted to the Opposition. Social-

Contd. on Back Page, Col. 4

He Will Feed Us

Lord Woolton becomes the new Minister for Food.

AIR MURDER MEN SAVED BY VICTIMS

FIVE German airmen in a Heinkel bomber were shot down and then saved by a British fishing crew they tried to murder yesterday.

The fishermen were in a little Scarborough drifter. Bullets from their Lewis gun finished off a job a Spitfire fighter had started. The Heinkel flopped on the sea.

"We couldn't do anything but rescue the Germans," said one of the drifter men. "They looked so helpless clinging to their sinking craft."

And the men who had fired burst after burst of machine-gun bullets at a few fishermen were hauled to safety by their victims.

Only one precaution the fishermen had to take. Five armed Germans were enough to overpower them.

"So the airmen were warned that it would be their last moment if they came aboard with revolvers," said a drifter man.

One of the Nazis was a wing-commander.

The fishermen had captured the highest ranking officer so far taken in air operations.

When the drifter reached port, one of the crew said that the German wing commander confided that he

Contd. on Back Page, Col. 3

FELL 30 FEET —APOLOGISED

FIFTEEN minutes after he had crashed to what seemed certain death, a London office boy was back at his desk as usual yesterday.

He is fifteen-year-old Edmund Finn of Sangley-road, S.E.6.

Edmund crashed through a skylight, fell 20ft. on to a banister rail, rebounded on to a wall, fell another 10ft. and rolled down a dozen stairs.

He then wiped his slightly-cut hand and, after apologising for the mess, walked off as if nothing had happened.

Edmund said: "My only worry was who was going to pay for the glass, and my greatest relief was to hear that it was insured. I felt worse coming down than when I stopped."

A GERMAN SOLDIER TELLS GERMANY

A Canadian soldier broadcast in German to Germany through the B.B.C. last night.

The soldier said he was born in Germany and left twelve years ago. "Like Hitler," he said, "I fought as a simple soldier in the German Army. I am convinced of another complete defeat for the German Army—unless Hitler and his gang are overthrown."

Fed and Watered

In 1939, most farms were mixed farms of between 50 and 250 acres and, although marketing boards existed and the price of wheat was guaranteed, the industry was still depressed. Out of 29 million acres of arable land, 17 million acres was permanent grassland.

The coming of war would forever change the face of British farming. Under the supervision of the County War Agricultural Executive Committees, farmers were paid a subsidy of £2 an acre to plough up grassland for crops. By the end of the war, nearly six million acres of what had been permanent grassland was under cultivation, some of it thanks to government financial assitance for drainage works and reclamation projects.

Farming became increasingly mechanised. At the outbreak of war, around 56,000 tractors were in use on UK farms, and by its end the number had risen to 203,000. Efficient use was made of combine harvesters, which were moved from farm to farm as they were needed. Between 1942 and 1945, the number of disc harrows in use more than doubled. There was also a massive increase in the use of fertilisers.

One lesser known function of the County War Agricultural Committee was to assess and classify farms according to productivity. Upon receiving a classification, a farmer could apply for assistance – usually in the form of WLA personnel – as well as equipment. Subsequently, if a farmer failed to comply with directives, he could in the worst-case scenario be evicted. The most famous, and the most tragic, case involved a Hampshire farmer who was ordered off his farm for failing to comply with a directive to plough four acres. The man refused to leave, and the police were called. Barricading himself in the farmhouse, the farmer opened fire with a sporting gun, wounding several officers. The police retaliated with tear gas but when that failed, armed reinforcements were sent for. They stormed the building shooting the farmer dead.

On a lighter note, depending on one's point of view, there is the interesting story of a farmer who showed initiative in finding dogs new owners.

At the start of the war, fear of immediate bombing and gas attacks resulted in many dog lovers having their pets destroyed.

Our friend advertised in newspapers offering to provide sanctuary for any number of dogs. Owners were told that once their pet had been found a new home that was it. They would never see their pet again though they were welcome to telephone or write and they would be provided with updates. Enquires were met with "Fido is enjoying living with some very nice people in Cumbria, well away from any bombing," or something to that effect. However, our farmer friend had contacts in the boot and shoe industry around Leicester and a by now very dead Fido was supplying the lining for fur-lined boots. What happened to the rest of Fido is unclear, though the same farmer had a reliable supply of under the counter off-ration sausages, no questions asked.

City farming 1943 style comes to London as pigs and rabbits are reared for food in a tumbledown building under the shadow of St Paul's. (*Mirrorpix*).

One way of supplementing official rations was by growing your own. Allotments sprang up everywhere from school playing fields to railway embankments. Even factories got in on the act. The Ford Merlin engine plant at Trafford Park, Manchester, took over sixteen acres of land adjacent to the site and used it to grow vegetables for the works canteen.

In July 1940, the *Nottingham Evening Post* was advising its readers to pay a visit to the Estates Department at the Guildhall, where an advisory bureau on gardens and allotments was being established. Land was being made available and the council were willing to come along and plough it. Council tenants, nearly all of whom had decent sized gardens, were encouraged to grow vegetables to the extent of digging up flower beds and lawns.

Being able to grow your own took on an importance all its own when then Acquisition of Food (Excessive Quantities) Order came into force. Officials were given powers to enter homes and inspect the contents of the larder.

If there was more than a week's ration, even by a small amount, the householder faced prosecution that could result in a fine and possible imprisonment. Bureaucratic eccentricity reached new heights when it was decreed that bread could no longer be served in cafes and restaurants at lunchtime. Notices appeared in all seriousness in the Press announcing the fact that Food Office officials would be mounting lightning raids on eating establishments to see what diners had on their side plates. It was completely barmy as bread was never rationed during the war.

During June 1941, tomatoes seemed to vanish from the shops. At the beginning of the month they were on sale at an average price of 2s. 6d (12.5p) per pound (approx. £6.35 in 2019) so few people were disposed to part with their hard-earned cash. By the third week in June, they had become subject to a control maximum retail price of 1s. 2d (6p) per pound and flew off the shelves.

Soon to be disappearing from a railway refreshment room near you. The ubiquitous railway ham sandwich – with or without curled edges and modestly priced at 4d – was one of the first wartime catering casualties. Its demise was announced in November 1939, though somewhat optimistically the powers that be promised to replace it with beef. The beef never arrived. (*Manchester Evening News*).

Before the war, tomatoes were imported in vast quantities from the Channel Islands and the Netherlands. Now, the country relied on home-grown produce and the crop was at least three weeks late due to frosts during May. They would be available in July, though not enough to satisfy demand.

In 1939, the UK produced 4.26 million tons of grains, increasing to 7.74 million tons in 1943. Over the same period, production of potatoes rose from 4.35 million tons to 8.54 million tons, whilst meat fell from 1.18 million tons to 754,000 tons.

(Right). The war on waste is the subject of this photograph from May 1941. Mrs. Worthless is caught red handed throwing all and sundry into the dustbin. Bread, potato peelings and other kitchen waste. The message was, "Many brave lives and boats have been lost bringing this food to you. Utilise this scrap now and save lives." (*Mirrorpix*).

Norman Fox, farmer cum bus driver, teaching the art of ploughing near Bellingham, Northumberland. April 1942. (*Mirrorpix*).

A Land Army girl ploughing on a farm in Berkshire. The image carries a file date of 11 November 1940. The Women's Land Army had reformed in June 1939 and was 20,000 strong by September 1941.

Apart from the uniform, they were not really an army at all. They worked long hours, the pay was poor, billeting often inadequate and leave virtually non-existent at just seven days a year. By June 1944, WLA strength stood at 80,000 and of these around 6000 were members of the Timber Corps, lumberjacking often in remote locations. (George Greenwell, *Daily Mirror*).

Sowing potatoes and feeding the pigs were just two of the jobs done by members of the Women's Land Army. Every pig in the UK had to be registered with the government and farmers were not allowed to slaughter one for their own use. They could kill an animal that had been seriously injured but, even then, the meat had to be accounted for. However, pigs and sheep had the habit of falling down holes in the ground and could not be recovered – the aroma of bacon frying or roast lamb coming from the farmhouse being purely coincidental.

There was one farmer who succeeded in rearing an unregistered a pig and, when the time came, he had it slaughtered along with a registered animal of about the same size by a butcher friend. All went well until it came to sending the registered animal to Derby Market. The fool sent two left sides.

In September 1940, the Ministry of Agriculture dropped a not too subtle hint that the way pigs were fed had to change. According to the ministry, it took 6.5 cwt (330 kg) of meal to produce 1.5 cwt (76 kg) of pig meat. Pigs had to get down to what they were naturally good at – eating waste as well as foraging in woodland. The policy was intended to push pig rearing away from relying on bulk feed. (*Daily Mirror*).

Farmers busy threshing. In 1940, troops helped bring in the harvest. (*Lincolnshire Echo*).

ARP allotments. (*Derby Telegraph*).

THIS PLAN WILL GIVE YOU YOUR OWN VEGETABLES ALL THE YEAR ROUND

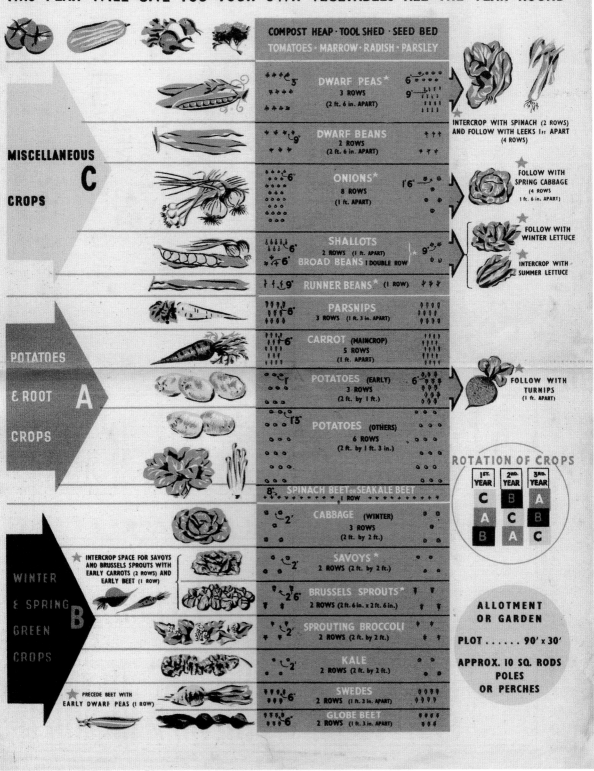

COMPOST HEAP · TOOL SHED · SEED BED
TOMATOES · MARROW · RADISH · PARSLEY

MISCELLANEOUS C CROPS

DWARF PEAS ★
3 ROWS
(2 ft. 6 in. APART)

INTERCROP WITH SPINACH (2 ROWS)
AND FOLLOW WITH LEEKS 1ft APART
(4 ROWS)

DWARF BEANS
2 ROWS
(2 ft. 6 in. APART)

ONIONS ★
8 ROWS
(1 ft. APART)

FOLLOW WITH
SPRING CABBAGE
(4 ROWS)
1 ft. 6 in. APART

SHALLOTS
2 ROWS (1 ft. APART)
BROAD BEANS 1 DOUBLE ROW

FOLLOW WITH
WINTER LETTUCE

INTERCROP WITH
SUMMER LETTUCE

RUNNER BEANS ★ (1 ROW)

PARSNIPS
3 ROWS (1 ft. 3 in. APART)

CARROT (MAINCROP)
5 ROWS
(1 ft. APART)

POTATOES & ROOT A CROPS

POTATOES (EARLY)
3 ROWS
(2 ft. by 1 ft.)

FOLLOW WITH
TURNIPS
(1 ft. APART)

POTATOES (OTHERS)
6 ROWS
(2 ft. by 1 ft. 3 in.)

SPINACH BEET or SEAKALE BEET
1 ROW

CABBAGE (WINTER)
3 ROWS
(2 ft. by 2 ft.)

INTERCROP SPACE FOR SAVOYS
AND BRUSSELS SPROUTS WITH
EARLY CARROTS (2 ROWS) AND
EARLY BEET (1 ROW)

SAVOYS ★
2 ROWS (2 ft. by 2 ft.)

BRUSSELS SPROUTS ★
2 ROWS (2 ft. 6 in. x 2 ft. 6 in.)

WINTER & SPRING GREEN CROPS B

SPROUTING BROCCOLI
2 ROWS (2 ft. by 2 ft.)

KALE
2 ROWS (2 ft. by 2 ft.)

★ PRECEDE BEET WITH
EARLY DWARF PEAS (1 ROW)

SWEDES
2 ROWS (1 ft. 3 in. APART)

GLOBE BEET
2 ROWS (1 ft. 3 in. APART)

ROTATION OF CROPS

1st YEAR	2nd YEAR	3rd YEAR
C	B	A
A	C	B
B	A	C

ALLOTMENT
OR GARDEN

PLOT ...... 90' x 30'

APPROX. 10 SQ. RODS
POLES
OR PERCHES

"ONLY 30/- A WEEK TO FEED FIVE"

This real-life story is based on the actual experiences of an Oxted family whose name and address can be seen on personal application.

Many other families are finding that
Rowntree's Cocoa makes every meal go further

(Above left). A strike by Manchester gas workers left some without a supply. Mrs. Margaret Jones, of New Bridge Street, commandeered the watchman's brazier at a nearby road works to cook on. 21 April 1944. (*Mirrorpix*). (Below). Bottling plums. (*Derby Telegraph*).

Coastal convoys under attack by the Luftwaffe in August 1940. The top image (*Daily Mirror*) was taken at Folkestone. At the outbreak of war, there were 1479 British registered coastal merchant ships totalling 1,151,880grt plying their trade around the UK, manned by 21,324 British and 261 foreign seamen.

When the Luftwaffe began its bombing campaign against London in September 1940, it was decided to close the Port of London to ocean-going merchant ships for several months. When this was relaxed in early 1941, restrictions were imposed as to the total number of these vessels allowed on the Thames at any one time.

Coasters came into their own during 1941 when ports south of the Humber were declared off limits to many ocean-going ships. This meant that ships that would have been bound for ports such as London, Harwich, Immingham during peacetime, were now discharging cargo at west coast ports such as Liverpool, Cardiff, and Bristol. As these cargoes still needed to reach their final destinations, a large proportion was transhipped to the railways. At Liverpool, about 12 per cent of cargo landed pre-war went onward by rail. By 1944 that figure had increased to 30 per cent. The advantage of using coastal shipping was that cargo could be transferred in almost any sheltered water as well as freeing up the railways. (*Mirrorpix*).

A FEW
CARELESS WORDS
MAY END IN THIS—

Many lives were lost in the last war through careless talk
Be on your guard ! Don't discuss movements of ships or troops

A cargo of dried beans being
unloaded at Liverpool. February 1942.
(Rueben Saidman. *Daily Herald*).

Catapult armed merchantmen (CAM) were an emergency stop-gap that provided convoys with limited air
cover in the shape of a single Hawker Hurricane fighter launched by means of a rocket-propelled launcher.
Once the enemy had been destroyed or driven off, the pilot had to ditch the aircraft in the sea and trust to
being picked up. In a convoy, the CAM, which also carried cargo, was stationed at the head of the outside
port column, allowing it plenty of space to turn into the wind to launch its aircraft. Thirty-five CAMs were used
and of these twelve were sunk. They were replaced by escort carriers. Some small merchant ships were fitted
out to fly barrage balloons to protect convoys from air attack. (*Mirrorpix*).

Trawlermen at work in the North Sea. The first British trawler to be sunk by enemy action during world war two was the Fleetwood-registered *Davara*. On the afternoon of 12 September 1939, when 21 miles NNW of Tory Island, County Donegal, she was shelled by U-27. The crew managed to get away in a lifeboat.

Just three days later, U-27 stopped and boarded the trawler *Rudyard Kipling*. The trawlermen were ordered to lower a lifeboat and make for the U-boat where they were taken on board. The U-boat boarding party then raided the trawler's food supplies and took away the wireless equipment. The trawler was then sunk by demolition charges.

The trawlermen remained on the U-boat for about eight hours and were well treated and fed. They were then put in their own lifeboat and released approximately five miles off the Donegal coast. The difference in the treatment these trawler crews received might have been because the commander of U-27 had been reminded that hostile action against merchant vessels had to be in accordance with the London Convention.

The bottom image shows a trawlerman taking cover during an attack by enemy aircraft. (*Mirrorpix*).

Entertainment and Sport

On the entertainment front, the BBC's fledgling television service was closed on 1 September 1939, but as so few people could either afford a set or receive the programmes it was hardly missed. Radio was another matter. By the outbreak of the war, most households either owned a wireless or had access to one.

On 3 September 1939, the BBC announced the reorganisation of the Home Service. A BBC in-house Repertory Company of thirty-six actors and actresses was to be formed including Carleton Hobbs, Thea Holme, Philip Wade, Patric Curwen and D.A. Clarke-Smith. As productions went out 'live' and to avoid expected disruption to travel, members of the Rep were billeted in the Concert Hall at Broadcasting House.

The Variety Department announced it would retain the services of such people as Tommy Handley, Leonard Henry and Doris Arnold, and the BBC Symphony Orchestra would continue with an establishment of seventy-five musicians. The Variety Department was relocated to Bristol and it was from there that, at 7.30pm on Tuesday, 19 September 1939, the first programme in a new series of what would become the most famous BBC radio show of all time was transmitted.

Four pilot shows of *ITMA – It's That Man Again* – had been broadcast the previous summer with Tommy Handley as the anchor man. The powers that be had decided that *ITMA* would be the ideal format for lampooning war in general and in particular the Nazi leadership. Handley played the Minister of Aggravation and Mysteries. Other characters were Mrs Mopp (Can I do you now, sir?) played by Doris Summers, while Fred Yule played Chief Bigga, Dino Galvani played Signor So-So, Jack Train played Colonel Chinstrap and Sydney Keith played Sam Scram. Each programme was a send-up of Radio Luxembourg, which had ceased transmitting at the outbreak of hostilities. Maurice Denholm would announce Radio Fakenburg and Sam Costa sang spoof commercials.

ITMA was given a regular 8.30pm Thursday night slot and repeated for the benefit of British forces overseas. Popular with listeners from all walks of life, Jack Train is supposed to have been told by a gentleman of the royal household that 'If the war were to end between 8.30-9.00pm on a Thursday night, none of the Household would dare tell the King until *ITMA* had finished.'

Other popular programmes were *Nether Backwash* starring Rob Wilton as the befuddled magistrate Mr. Muddlecombe and the variety show Garrison Theatre featuring Jack Warner. Wing Commander Kenneth Horne and stand-up comic corporal Bill Waddington, who would go on to play Percy Sugden in *Coronation Street*, featured in the show, '*Ack-Ack Here*.' Horne also featured alongside Squadron Leader Richard 'Stinker' Murdoch and Eric Barker in *Much Binding in the Marsh*, a comedy set on a RAF station. In the show Horne and Murdoch often sang duets under the name *The Stinkpots*. Husband and wife team Ben Lyon and Bebe Daniels starred in the hit show *Hi Gang!* and then *Life with the Lyons*.

The country's highest-paid entertainer and top box office star George Formby entertains Londoners sheltering in Aldwych tube station on 10 November 1940. During the year, George had released twelve records the most famous being his recording of *Bless 'Em All* (The Long and the Short and the Tall), as well as starring in the feature films *Let George Do It!* and *Spare a Copper*. (*Daily Mirror*).

On 23 June 1940, the BBC began broadcasting *Music While You Work*, described in the Radio Times as a 'half hour's music meant specially for factory workers to listen to as they work.' With the country's industry now on a war footing and working round the clock, *Music While You Work* was broadcast twice daily.

Also aired for the first time in June 1940 was *Workers' Playtime*, a variety show broadcast from a works canteen 'Somewhere in England.' Compered by Bill Gates, the early programmes followed a set format; piano medley, a culture slot featuring a tenor or soprano, and finishing off with a comedian and a bit of a sing-along. Regular acts included comedy turns from Harry Champion, Billy Kaye, Tony Fame, Robb Wilton, Elsie and Doris Waters and Claude Dampier. The show proved an instant success and during the following October it was broadcast three times a week. From June 1942, midnight broadcasts entered the schedules for the benefit of those working nights and to allow transmission to the USA.

More serious fare was dished up in the form of concerts and talks. On New Year's Day 1941, a new programme in which listeners' questions were answered by a panel of experts was initially broadcast on the Forces Programme under the title *Any Questions*. The panellists were the philosopher and psychologist Professor Cyril Joad, the biologist Julian Huxley, and retired Royal Navy officer Commander A.B. Campbell, with Donald McCullogh in the chair. From the second series onwards, the programme was retitled *The Brains Trust*. It soon proved so popular that it was given the Home Service's prime Sunday afternoon slot and its initial run lasted 84 weeks.

Much airtime was devoted to dance band music, some of the favourites being Billy Cotton, Joe Loss, Jack Hylton and Henry Hall. Popular singers included Gracie Fields, Vera Lynn, and Ann Shelton. When the American Forces Network went on air, listeners were treated to the big band sound of Tommy Dorsey, jazz from Benny Carter and the singing talents of Ella Fitzgerald and a young man

The Terry Cantor ENSA concert party, November 1940. Born Kenneth Edward McNaughton in Sheffield in 1912, his career as a comedian and actor continued into the 1970s when he appeared in TV series such as *All Creatures Great and Small*, *Oh No, It's Selwyn Froggitt*, *Queenie's Castle* and *Follyfoot*. He died in Palma, Mallorca, in 1979. (*Derby Telegraph*).

by the name of Frank Sinatra. American comedians such as Bob Hope, Jack Benny and Red Skelton managed to bridge the cultural and language differences between the two countries, proving extremely popular with British listeners.

Of all the band music of the time, it is probably the tunes of Glenn Miller that have become synonymous with the war years. With hit records such as *Moonlight Serenade*, *Tuxedo Junction*, *Little Brown Jug* and *Pennsylvania 6-5000* to his credit, Miller surprised everyone when he enlisted in the US army in 1942. Given responsibility for organizing service bands, Miller came to England in June 1944 and gave a series of concerts. On 15 December, he boarded a single-engine UC-64A Norseman at RAF Twinwood Farm near Bedford for France. The plane took off into the mist and was never seen again. Miller's disappearance was not announced until Christmas Eve, when the Press Association made public the fact that he would not be conducting the AEF Christmas Show, scheduled to be broadcast by the BBC.

In January 2019, a possible wreck site of Miller's aircraft, thirty miles south of Portland Bill, was scheduled for investigation. Wreckage was caught in a fishing net in 1987 but cut loose, though the fisherman recorded its location which is on the flight path Miller's plane would have taken.

So much for radio, what about theatres and cinema? On Friday 1 September 1939, the people of Grimsby had a wide selection of variety shows, cinema and dances to choose from - not only around the town but also in nearby Cleethorpes. At the Regal, the main picture was *King of the Underworld* staring Humphrey Bogart and Kay Francis, followed after the intermission by Penny Singleton and Arthur Lake in the hilarious Blondie comedy, *Blondie Meets the Boss*.

At the *Savoy*, Alastair Sim and Gordon Harker were appearing in *Inspector Hornleigh*, a film adaptation of a radio sleuth. The supporting movie was Jane Withers in *Miss Fix-It*. The Savoy was one of those great 1930s picture houses that had a café. Open from 11am till 10.15 pm, it served light refreshments, afternoon tea, snacks, and grills, all at reasonable prices.

Other movies showing around Grimsby that weekend included, *Mr Moto's Last Warning* starring Peter Lorre, Angels With Dirty Faces starring James Cagney and Pat O'Brien, *Spawn of the North* starring George Raft, Dorothy Lamour

The Hotspurs Concert Party travelled around the North East putting on performances in their mobile theatre. October 1940. (Charlie Ley, *Daily Mirror*).

and Henry Fonda, and *Hard to Get* starring Dick Powell and Olivia De Havilland.

At the Tivoli Theatre, John D Robertson was presenting his latest Topical Review, *Everybody's Doing It,* featuring Angus Watson, Jack Lewis and His Rolling Stones, Dolly Lewis, Edith Wallington, and the Jay Dee Girls. However, the Café Dansant was the place to be for those who fancied their chances for five minutes of fame. Friday night was grand late carnival night, complete with a crooning competition and a jitterbug contest.

Over at Cleethorpes, 6d would buy you a seat at the Olympia (opposite the bus terminus) for the *Olympian Follies,* 'ten first class acts in a happy holiday revue.' Complete change of programme every Monday. At the Royal, Pat O'Brien and Joan Blondell were starring in *Off the Record*, though cinemagoers for the second house could watch Mr Taylor-Brown, managing editor of the *Evening Telegraph,* and the mayor and mayoress present the Beauty Queen prizes.

At the Empire, Max Miller and Chili Bouchier were appearing in the movie *Everything Happens to Me*, a fast-moving "Cheekie Chappie" musical comedy, and the Pier Pavilion was advertising the Lincolnshire Summer Amateur Dancing Competition. The first preliminary heat was scheduled for Monday 4 September, the winners to receive a silver challenge cup.

Immediately following Neville Chamberlain's broadcast on Sunday 3 September 1939, the Government announced the immediate closure of all places of entertainment as well as all indoor and outdoor sports gatherings. The closure was to last until further notice. It was a precautionary measure aimed at reducing possible casualties in the event of air raids. The measure would be kept under review with the possibility that some cinemas and theatres might be able to reopen in some areas should events allow it.

Even so, Denham Studios soon had the country's first war film in production. Starring Ralph Richardson and Merle Oberon, *The Lion Has Wings* was in cinemas before there had been any air raids. It was produced by Alexander Korda, a good friend of Winston Churchill. Korda promised to have a feature length propaganda film on general release within one month of the declaration

Bud Flanagan and Chesney Allen. Famed for such songs as *Run Rabbit Run*, *Underneath the Arches*, and *We're Going to Hang out the Washing on the Siegfried Line*. Shortly before his death in 1968, Bud recorded *Who Do You Think You Are Kidding Mister Hitler* for the TV comedy series *Dad's Army*. (*Mirrorpix*).

Max Miller on stage doing his solo act. From December 1939 to July 1940, he appeared along with Vera Lynn in the revue *Apple Sauce* at the Holborn Empire. Risque jokes and flamboyant suits were his trademark. By 1943, Max was earning more than £1000 (£45,939.52p in 2019) a week. (*Mirrorpix*).

of war. The movie relied on cobbled together stock film as well as some location filming at RAF bases at Hornchurch and Mildenhall.

When places of entertainment reopened, patrons were to be refused admission if they were not carrying gas masks. A cinema manager in Newcastle upon Tyne claimed that after performances his cinema was littered with impromptu 'containers' holding half bricks and wastepaper, the punters having abandoned their 'respirators.'

Toward the end of September 1940, a twelve-year-old boy from Herne Hill, London, was evacuated to the US along with his mother and sister. On 14 November, several papers were reporting that the boy, Roderick Andrew (Roddy) McDowell, had landed a part in the Hollywood movie *How Green Was My Valley*. Roddy, already a child actor, had appeared in sixteen British movies including *This England*, *I See Ice* and *Saloon Bar* as well as the Will Hay films *Convict 99* and *Hey! Hey! USA*. His success at landing the part was due in no small circumstance to the fact he already knew the book and his family's Welsh maid in London had taught him Welsh accents. The film won the Academy Award for Best Picture.

On 19 March 1940, the audience at the London Pavilion saw flames projected on the screen during a showing of *Two Bright Boys*. It was not some portent of doom. The gate of the projector had jammed, and a piece of film caught fire. The projectionist quickly spliced the film and the show went on. In London, the most famous theatre of the war was the naughty but nice *Windmill* and its nude tableaux. The theatre ran continuous performances from 2.30pm till 11pm. During the war, the *Windmill* proudly boasted "We Never Closed," which apart from the compulsory closure of all places of entertainment between 4-16 September 1939, is true – even at the height of the London blitz.

The nude tableaux were the brainchild of Vivian Van Damm and included such delicacies as *Mermaids*, *Annie Oakley* and *Red Indians*. Van Damm was also responsible for choreographing the Windmill fan dance. Providing the ladies in the tableaux did not move, it was not considered rude. The theatre was also home to the Windmill Steeplechase, the name given to the chaos at the end of each performance when the patrons at the back of the theatre rushed forward to occupy seats vacated nearer the stage. When owner Laura Henderson died in November 1944, aged 82, she left the *Windmill* to Vivian Van Damm.

"You lucky people." Tommy Trinder makes an appearance at Leicester Square during War Weapons Week, March 1943. During the Blitz on London, theatre audiences were required to remain in their seats. It was during one such raid that Trinder drove from theatre to theatre offering to do a ten-minute spot in each. By the time the all-clear sounded, Trinder had given no fewer than seventeen different performances.

From the very start of the war, Trinder had gone out of his way to entertain service personnel stationed in the UK, and while his material could get earthy, he never resorted to crudity. In 1943 he was unjustly singled out for criticism in the House of Commons. His crime was he had not worked overseas for ENSA. He was, however, the first major British star to tour Italy and in 1946 he topped the bill of the last ENSA show in the Far East. (*Mirrorpix*).

Mrs Laura Henderson, owner of the *Windmill Theatre,* with the *Revudebelles*, the ladies who appeared in the theatre's famous, or infamous, nude tableaux vivants. (*Mirrorpix*).

A film of the popular radio comedy show *Hi Gang!* starring Bebe Daniels and Ben Lyon was made by Gainsborough Pictures at their Lime Grove Studios, West London. Also appearing were Moore Marriott and Graham Moffatt in one of their first films since the dissolution of their partnership with Will Hay. The film was released in the UK on 27 December 1941. (*Mirrorpix*).

The ATS band was formed in 1941 at the No.14 Recruit Training Centre, Droitwich, when Junior Commander Angela Stebbing who was serving there called for musically-minded volunteers to step forward. The outcome was an eighteen-strong drum and bugle band which soon proved popular, performing at parades throughout the UK. The band's HQ eventually moved to Gower Street, London, and in January 1944 the unit was awarded full military band status and its strength raised to fifty-five. A pipe band was also added.

At the England v Scotland international football match at Wembley on 16 October 1944, music was provided by the band of the Scots Guards who played for Scotland, and the full military band and pipes of the ATS who played for England.

The ATS Dance Band played venues around London including the London Casino, Old Compton Street. They regularly featured on Forces Radio and shows such as *Workers Play Time* and *Variety Band Box*.

The ATS band ceased to exist in 1946 when most of its members were demobbed. (*Mirrorpix*).

(Below). The full regimental band of the ATS parades through Derby. At the time, it was thought that this was the first all ladies' band to have given a concert in the Market Place. Shoppers and other pedestrians lined the route of the band's march from the Midland station, then via London Road, St Peter's Street, the Cornmarket and on to the Market Place. 29 September 1944. (*Derby Telegraph*).

Belle Vue, Manchester, played a pivotal role in the area's 'Holidays at Home' campaign. It was one of only a handful of venues of this type allowed to remain open even though the war proved to be a difficult time as restrictions impacted heavily on its activities. Crowd-pulling events such as the firework displays were cancelled and some of the fairground rides mothballed. The Christmas Circus continued though it was restricted to afternoon performances only. After the Manchester Free Trade Hall was destroyed by bombing, the Kings' Hall at Belle Vue became the home of the Halle Orchestra.

Belle Vue Zoo became a refuge for animals evacuated from zoos forced to close. Unfortunately, those species reliant on food supplies from overseas suffered through lack of availability and subsequently many died. Belle Vue's penguin population was wiped out through lack of fish and the sea lions developed stomach ulcers from consuming beef soaked in cod liver oil. Also, the entire collection of tropical fish died when the heating system failed due to a disruption in the gas supplies. The monkeys lived on boiled potatoes and the lions were fed horse meat, though the regulations required it to be marked with a harmless green dye.

One direct casualty of the bombing was a bull bison killed by splinters from an anti-aircraft shell. Splinters from anti-aircraft rounds also damaged the Reptile House, and keepers were armed with rifles as a precaution to prevent animals escaping should the zoo be hit by bombs.

Many animals have hearing more acute than humans and keepers reported that they showed signs of distress during air raids even when the raids were many miles away.

The facilities at Belle Vue was also used for training purposes by the military. (*Manchester Evening News*).

On Friday 1 September 1939, the Football League announced that for the time being matches would go-ahead though the President of the League, William Cuff, urged clubs to keep their ears open for wireless and Press announcements. However, due to the international situation, the county cricket match between Lancashire and Surrey at Old Trafford was abandoned. Of the county cricket matches played, Yorkshire beat Sussex by nine wickets, Verity destroying Sussex's second innings by taking seven wickets for just nine runs. Worcestershire beat Notts by an innings and 31 runs; Somerset beat Northants by an innings and 92 runs; Middlesex thrashed Warwickshire by an innings and 200 runs, and the game between Leicestershire and Derbyshire was abandoned as a draw due to the sodden condition of the pitch. The match between Middlesex and Kent at Lords which had been scheduled to start the following day was cancelled.

On 6 September, the Football League Management Committee met at Crewe. With a Government ban in place under the Defence Regulations on all spectator sports likely to attract crowds, the committee officially suspended the League and released all players from their contracts. Eight days later, the Government gave the go-ahead for friendly matches providing there were no objections from local police forces.

To complete the 1939-40 season, the English Football League reorganised its four divisions into six regional ones: North West, South Western, Midland, East Midland, North Eastern, South (C), and South (D). The Scottish Leagues were reorganised into Eastern and Western Divisions. It was agreed that players should be allowed to turn out for the side nearest to where they were working, or, if in the armed forces, nearest to where they were stationed. However, by April 1940, the wartime cup competition was causing problems as some clubs, anxious to have their registered players available, refused permission for them to play for other teams. For example, Charlton Athletic would not allow their centre

Soldiers watching a League football match. September 1939. (*Mirrorpix*).

forward Maurice Tadman to play in a cup tie for Bristol Rovers. In the Leagues it was business as usual. When West Ham United entertained Arsenal, the Hammers had only ten players available, so Gunners' manager George Allison lent them inside left George (Twinkletoes) Curtis. The Hammers won 2-1.

Even by December 1939, some wartime League football was suffering. Torquay United and Newport County were struggling and there were doubts they would be able to continue unless gates increased. When Torquay entertained Bristol City on 2 December, Bristol's share of the gate had been so small that they lost £25 (£1646 in 2019) on the trip, whilst the Football League's share was a colossal 1s. 6d (7.5p).

Some fans were also unhappy. Henry Dilworth, of Arkwright Street, Bolton, brought a case against Bolton wanderers demanding a refund of 15s on his season ticket because he unable to see the League games he had paid for. It was something

of a test case for the entire Football League. If the case went against Bolton, clubs could face demands for the return of thousands of pounds worth of season ticket sales. As it was, Judge Crosthwaite said that the moment the war made football impossible, Dilworth was unable to recover his money because the contract became impossible due to an order under the Defence Regulations making it illegal. Season ticket holders were allowed into regional League matches.

On the other hand, the Army was having no problem fielding strong sides. Among the players available for the match against Scotland on 24 April 1940 were Frank Swift (Manchester City), Joe Mercer (Everton), Stan Cullis (Wolves), Matt Busby (Liverpool), Tommy Lawton (Everton), and Dennis Compton (Arsenal).

Preston North End lift the 1941 Football League Cup having held Arsenal to a draw at Wembley and winning the replay 2-1 at Ewood Park. Wolverhampton Wanderers were winners in 1942 after which the competition was organised on a regional basis, League Cup North, League Cup South, and League Cup West. (*Daily Mirror*).

In May 1939, Bolton Wanderers players enlisted en masse in the Territorial Army. Serving with the 53rd Field Regiment, Royal Artillery, the men continued to play football together as an army side. During December 1939, they returned to Bolton on Christmas leave, and as an Army XI played against a wartime Bolton Wanderers line-up at Burden Park. Only 1509 spectators turned up to watch the thrill-a-minute 3-3 draw. (Crown, *Daily Herald*).

Charlton Athletic v Reading at the Valley on 26 August 1944. (Edwin Appleton. *Daily Herald*).

Training session for the Fairey Aviation Co. ladies football team. The side played against teams from ATS and WAAF units in the surrounding area. (*Mirrorpix*).

In February 1940, Sussex announced that for the coming season they would not play any matches requiring payments to professional players. From a financial point of view, the 1939 season had not been thrilling. The club recorded a net loss of £1853 (£104,511 in 2019). The August Bank Holiday match against Middlesex had been wrecked by the weather and the outbreak of war had seen the West Indies cancel the Annual Cricket Week game. The committee hoped to arrange one or two-day friendlies against neighbouring counties as well as matches against Sussex public schools. As the club's liabilities for 1940 were estimated at £2500 (£141,000 in 2019), the committee were hoping members would open their wallets.

One of the great interwar period spectator sports was greyhound racing, many tracks holding four meetings a week. Introduced from the USA in 1926, greyhound racing was an instant hit with the working class as they too could own and race dogs. When racing resumed, the tracks were each limited to one afternoon meeting a week.

During the winter months, a razor blade, a bottle of Indian ink, a pen, and a steady hand, was all a felon needed to work the Tote scam. The Tote was reduced to using glorified raffle tickets, and, if the winning number was a 0,3,6,8, or 9, it was easy enough to scratch off the offending portion and alter a 0 to a 6, or a 9 to an 8 and so on. The Tote clerks often had little chance of spotting a fake as ARP regulations meant they worked under subdued lighting. Tracks soon became associated with spivs and dodgy deals and were frequently raided by military and civil police looking for deserters. Punters were rounded up and ID checks carried out.

On a lighter note, 1 September 1939, was the day 21-year-old Miss Marguerite Wilson, a professional cyclist with Hercules Cycle & Motor Co, set a new record for 'End-to-End' the 870-mile run between Land's End and John o' Groats. She completed the route in two days, 22 hours and 52 minutes, beating the previous record set in 1938 by Lilian Dredge of three days, 20 hours and 54 minutes.

Men versus women AFS match on 27 September 1941. The *Daily Mirror* later carried a story of how cricket helped mothers to give birth when a young nurse, Miss Randall, who by 1943 was sister-in-charge of midwifery at St Thomas's, went to a Varsity cricket match and was intrigued by the movements of the wicketkeeper.

"Sometimes he would have his hands on his knees, then he would rise to half upright position and so on. I realised that these movements must make the spine flexible and at the same time expand the pelvis. The whole idea is that a baby should be born with plenty of room so that it doesn't get squeezed. These exercises derived from what I saw at Lord's do the trick." (*Daily Mirror*).

The National Hunt classics race The Derby, was transferred from Epsom to Newmarket for the duration of the war where it was run under the name the New Derby. However, during July 1943, it did not stop Epsom & Ewell running a Pony Derby as part of their Wings for Victory Week.

The race was featured on a *Pathe* newsreel introduced by the actor and racehorse owner Tom Walls. Walls introduced with jockeys in turn starting with six-times Derby winner Steve Donoghue. The only one of the seven not to have won the classic was none other than the Champion Jockey, Gordon Richards, and he would have to wait until 1953 when he did it on *Pinza*.

The lady on the left of the image, looking like an escapee from an Old Mother Riley identification parade, is Kate. It was a nod to Old Kate, for several decades a tipster and well-known character at Epsom racecourse, who sadly was no longer around. Kate is holding Old Kate's original shooting stick, which was to be auctioned after the race, the proceeds going to the Wings for Victory fund.

The jockeys are left to right: Michael Beary, Tommy Carey, Charlie Elliot, Steve Donoghue, E Smith, Fred Lane, and Gordon Richards.

Cheered on by 10,000 spectators, the three-furlong race won by E Smith on *Stand at Ease*. The horse was owned by the Reverend Mother Veronica. (George Greenwell, *Daily Mirror*).

The home of Welsh rugby, Cardiff Arms Park, was just one of many sporting venues to be damaged by bombing. Among them were Manchester United's ground at Old Trafford, and Sheffield United's ground at Bramall Lane (*Western Mail Archive*).

Boxing match held on board the troopship RMS *Queen Mary* at Liverpool, 15 October 1941. The photographer climbed the mast to take the photograph. (*Liverpool Echo*).

Anyone for tennis? A Morrison shelter doubles up as a games table. 1 September 1941. (Official. *Mirrorpix*).

Don't Panic!

At 9.30am on 4 June 1940, the rear guard covering the withdrawal of British and Allied troops from the beaches of Dunkirk surrendered. Operation Dynamo as the evacuation had been codenamed was at an end. Though instead of the 20-30,000 troops expected to be brought back to Britain, the Royal Navy with a lot of help from civilian boat owners and the French Navy, had brought back 336,427 men. Even so, 90,000 troops were taken prisoner and the British Expeditionary Force had been forced to abandon most of its heavy equipment and artillery.

That day, Prime Minister Winston Churchill addressed Parliament and asked that the deliverance not be hailed as a victory. 'Wars are not won by evacuations,' he said. The fight would continue, though with the threat of invasion now hanging over Britain, there was an urgent need to redeploy regular troops to anti invasion duties.

A few weeks earlier on 14 May, Anthony Eden, the newly appointed Secretary of State for War, made a nationwide broadcast on the BBC. The German invasion of France and the Low Countries was under way. It was a new way of fighting and things were not going well for the Allies.

"I want to speak to you tonight about the form of warfare the Germans have been employing so extensively against Holland and Belgium – namely the dropping of troops by parachute behind the main defensive lines. Let me say at once that the danger to us from this particular menace, although it undoubtedly exists, should not be exaggerated. We have made preparations to meet it already.

"Let me describe to you the system under which these parachute raids are carried out. The troops arrive by aeroplane – but let it be remembered any such aeroplane seeking to penetrate here would do so in the teeth of the Anti-Aircraft defences of this country. If such penetration is effected, the parachutists are then dropped, it may be by day, it may be by night. These troops are specially armed, equipped, and some of them have undergone specialised training. Their function is to seize important points, such as aerodromes, power stations, villages, railway junctions and telephone exchanges, either for the purpose of destroying them at once, or holding them until

the arrival of reinforcements. The purpose of the parachute attack is to disorganise and confuse, as a preparation to the landing of troops by aircraft.

"The success of such an attack depends on speed. Consequently, the measures to defeat such an attack must be prompt and rapid. It is upon this basis that our plans have been laid. You will not expect me to tell you, or the enemy, what our plans are, but we are confident that they will be effective. However, in order to leave nothing to chance and to supplement, from sources yet untapped, the means of defence already arranged, we are going to ask you to help us, in a manner which I know will be welcome to thousands of you. Since the war began the Government have received countless enquiries from all over the Kingdom from men of all ages who are for one reason or another not at present engaged in military service, and who wish to do something for the defence of the country.

"Now is your opportunity. We want large numbers of men in Great Britain who are British subjects between the ages of 17 and 65 to come forward now and offer their services in order to make assurance doubly sure. The name of the new force which is now to be raised will be the Local Defence Volunteers. This name, Local Defence Volunteers, describes its duties in three words. It must be understood that this is, so to speak, a spare-time job, so there will be no need for any volunteer to abandon his present occupation.

"Part-time members of existing civil defence organisations should ask their officers' advice before registering under the scheme. men who will ultimately become due for calling up under the National Service (Armed Forces) Act may join temporarily and will be released to join the Army when they are required to serve. Now a word to those who propose to volunteer. When on duty you will form part of the Armed Forces, and your period of service will be for the duration of the war.

You will not be paid but you will receive uniforms and be armed. You will be entrusted with certain vital duties, for which reasonable fitness and a knowledge of firearms are necessary. These duties will not require you to live away from your homes. In order to volunteer, what you have to do is to give your name at your local police station; and then, as and when we want you, we will let you know.

"This appeal is directed chiefly to those who live in small towns, villages and less densely inhabited suburban areas. I must warn you that, for certain military reasons, there will be some localities where the numbers required will be small, and others where your services will not be required at all. Here then is the opportunity for which many of you have been waiting. Your loyal help, added to the arrangements which already exist, will make and keep our country safe."

The LDV unit at St Martin's Preserves, Cordwallis Works, Maidenhead, get in a dinner time training session accompanied by their homemade armoured car, nicknamed *Tickler's Tank* after company director Colonel W M Tickler. It was constructed out of sheet metal salvaged from scrapyards and a Sunbeam car chassis. Works manager, P A J Hammett, served in the ranks as a private. The LDV unit at the company's factory in Ely also had its own armoured car. (*Mirrorpix*).

Within minutes of Eden's broadcast the first volunteers were reporting in at local police stations to enrol. Those under the age limit added a year or two, those over the age limit shed a few years. At first, units were mainly those formed by employees to protect their own works premises though they were quickly followed by village, town, and city formations. Units were also formed to patrol navigable rivers using cabin cruisers and speed boats.

One of the early instructions issued to LDV units concerned the use of shotguns and sporting cartridges. These items were defined as legal weapons for use against enemy paratroops 'but only if used by properly enrolled members of the LDV.' Therefore, one must assume that an ordinary citizen taking a potshot at a passing Nazi was liable to prosecution. The first item of clothing received by LDV units was a stencilled armband, the first pieces of kit were whistles and broom handles or pike staffs, though those going out on patrol carried an assortment of weaponry including sporting guns, swords, battleaxes, clubs and Zulu assegai. One Lancashire unit had six spears with which to fend off any Nazis dropping from the sky.

Veterans of the Boer and Great Wars brought experience of battle to the ranks although few could equal eighty-year-old Alex Taylor from Perthshire. He had served in the Egyptian Campaign of 1884-85 and had taken part in the attempt to relieve General Gordon at Khartoum.

On 23 July, the LDV – already christened the 'look, duck and vanish' - was renamed the Home Guard and the following day their second piece of kit would soon be issued – army boots. Over the following weeks, units were issued with battledress uniforms, though more importantly a large shipment of rifles and Thompson sub machine guns arrived from the United States. They were distributed to units throughout the UK, men waiting for hours to receive them and volunteers working round-the-clock to make them operational. The Home Guard could now transfer its 30,000 British type .303 rifles and ammunition to the regular army.

Home Guard units were soon affiliated to local county regiments and regular NCOs were tasked with weapons training.

The pre-arranged signal for a paratroop landing was to be the ringing of church bells upon receipt of the codewords Operation Cromwell. On 7 September, the codeword was issued by HQ Home Command, not because an invasion had occurred but because one was deemed likely at any time. On learning that Operation Cromwell had been issued, some local commanders commandeered churches and ordered the bells rung.

The fledgling Home Guard stood to, ready to do its stuff even if ammunition was in short supply. Cromwell was lifted after twelve days, by which time the country was rife with rumours that an amphibious landing had been repulsed by setting the sea ablaze with flaming oil, barbecuing Germans in their assault craft.

By the summer of 1943, Home Guard strength stood at 1.75 million men in 1100 battalions. The organisation was being increasingly used to give 16 and 17-year-olds a taste of the army before call-up. Gone were the broom shanks, 12-bore shotguns and assorted cutlery from long-forgotten colonial wars. They had been replaced by increasingly sophisticated weapons.

One of the endearing qualities of the Home Guard was that it stood Britain's up-tight social and class structure on its head. The War Office insisted that promotions had to be on merit and not class or education, which meant a factory manager might well find himself ordered around by one of his labourers because the labourer happened to be a competent ex-soldier.

There are lots of true stories that might well have found their way into the scripts of *Dad's Army*.

The two 17-year olds out on patrol one night. They had a rifle but only one round of ammunition. One grabbed the arm of the other shouting "Look Harry, paratroops in that field!" Sure enough the field appeared to have white areas that might be parachutes. Suddenly, there was a rustling sound from a nearby hedge. Harry, the one with the rifle shouted, "Who goes there, identify yourself!" No answer, just more rustling. Harry fired and they both ran off. They reported back that there were paratroops. A patrol went to investigate, and the nearest regular army unit put on alert. The white turned out to be lime while behind the hedge lay the farmer's prize bull shot clean through its heart.

Then there was the platoon due to be inspected by a 'brass hat' from Catterick. The men paraded in front of a pub, full kit, bayonets fixed. They waited, and waited, and waited.

No sign of a staff car. That is until the pub opened whereupon an orderly retreat was made to the bar. While sipping their pints, the men saw a staff car pass along the street, its occupants searching in vain for the parade.

On another occasion, a unit decided to test fire its Blacker Bombard mortar. The weapon was set up and aimed towards a wood which supposedly had been cleared in advance. The mortar bomb did not contain an explosive charge, the idea being to retrieve it afterwards. The bomb landed near the middle of the wood and out of the woods shot a pair of flustered young lovers.

Bristol Evening Post chief photographer Jim Facey makes his way through the ranks of the 7th Somerset (Long Ashton) Battalion, Home Guard. There is no file date for the image, but it cannot be before early 1941 as some of the men are armed with Mk II Sten guns which could be set to fire automatically or single shots. Designed by Enfield and cheap and simple to make, many were manufactured by toy maker Tri-ang. The main drawback was that the barrel had to be held to steady the weapon and it soon got too hot to hold. The Home Guard were trained to use the weapon at ranges up to 40ft (12.1metres).

The 7th Battalion later provided recruits to the 101st and 104th batteries of Bristol's Z anti-aircraft rocket sites. (*Bristol Evening Post*).

Members of the Newcastle Home Guard. 13 August 1940. (*Newcastle Chronicle & Journal*).

Members of the Reading Home Guard check a motorist's identity papers during an anti-invasion exercise held in July 1941. (Valpy Street. *Reading Post*). (Below). German reconnaissance photograph of Henley on Thames. (Collection Clive Hardy).

Abb. 3. Blick themseabwärts nach N auf **Henley**. Oben der bewaldete SO-Abhang der Chiltern-Hills.

One of a series of images taken by the *Daily Mirror* in the early months of 1941, showing the preparedness of the Home Guard. The images featured members of the Home Guard around Dover and Folkstone. Here, sergeant major V Hollness and his sons are getting ready for duty. (*Daily Mirror*).

A temporary roadblock thrown across High Street, Abergwili, during an invasion exercise held in 1942. The Wheaten Sheaf Inn still stands (2020) and still sells Felinfoel Ales. In December 1935, Felinfoel beat rival brewery Buckley's in the race to produce beer in cans, though the fact that Felinfoel owned its own tinplate works probably helped. The beer was canned by the half pint and packed in cases of 24. Its lighter weight relative to glass made it ideal for sending to forces personnel stationed overseas. (*Western Mail*).

Home Guardsmen armed with sticky bombs capture an 'enemy' tank during an exercise. The image carries a file date of 23 May 1943. Though taken by a *Liverpool Echo* photographer, the location is not recorded. (*Liverpool Echo*).

Twelve armoured trains were formed in 1940 as part of the anti-invasion preparations. The locomotives were provided by the LNER, the wagons were built at the LMS Carriage & Wagon Works, Derby. The trains patrolled coastal lines in Scotland, Northumberland, Durham, Yorkshire, and Lincolnshire. The trains were heavily armed, each mounting two 6-pounder (57mm) Hotchkiss guns, six Bren guns, two Vickers .303 machine guns, and four Thompson sub-machine guns as well as the rifles and grenades carried by their crews. Soon placed under Free Polish Armed Forces operation, the trains were divided into four battalions, each consisting of three trains.

During 1942 the trains were handed over to the Home Guard. Though as the threat of invasion gradually receded, all but the three operating in Scotland (trains K, L and J) were withdrawn from service. In September 1944, as locomotive No.7573 of armoured train K was due its five-yearly overhaul at Stratford, London, the decision was taken to withdraw all of them from service. February 1944. (Official, *Daily Mirror*).

The Trent River Patrol of the Nottinghamshire Home Guard was formed in May 1940 and by the time this picture was taken in February 1943 it controlled just under 100 miles of inland waterways. Several motor launches, some armed with Vickers machine guns, were stationed at intervals along the River Trent. (*Mirrorpix*).

Home Guard patrol on Lake Windermere, one of the country's largest lakes. A twenty-four hours, seven days a week patrol was mounted using speed boats and cabin cruisers armed with machine guns. The main objective was to prevent the lake being used by enemy seaplanes. September 1943. (Official, *Mirrorpix*).

Toward the end of 1941, the decision was taken to transfer the manning of AA batteries to the Home Guard and in doing so release around 50,000 men for other duties. As well as light and heavy guns, the Home Guard would also take over the manning of Z batteries - short range, solid fuel, 3inch (76mm) AA rockets. The Z batteries were a recent development following successful trials toward the end of 1940 at an experimental site at Cardiff. Home Guard recruits were, wherever possible, allocated to the nearest battery to where they lived and worked.

At Bristol, recruitment began in February 1942, its units to be attached to the 9th AA 'Z' Regiment, Royal Artillery. By 26 June, Bristol's Z sites had formed 102 (Gloucestershire) HG Battery, with 101 Battery at Easton in Gordan, 103 at Brislington, and 104 at Abbots Leigh.

The Sheffield Gun Defended Area had 185 twin projectors dispersed over three sites. They were manned on a rota system by about 5400 men. Because it was necessary to work to a strict rota, men on shifts were not allowed to take part. It was also a requirement that the men who worked on Z batteries were physically fit and had good eyesight so they could lift the heavy projectiles and set the fuses accurately. Though the maximum age for recruits was 60, it was 40 for conventional AA guns and coast defence batteries.

The rockets were usually fired in salvoes of 100 at a time, each one accelerating to more than 1000 mph (1609.34 kph) in less than a second and a half. In doing so they made a tremendous noise. Fuses were set at 3500 feet (1066.8 metres) for dive bombers and 20,000 feet (6096 metres) for bombers.

On 3 March 1943, civilians queueing for the night shelter at Bethnal Green tube station were panicked by the noise of a newly installed Z battery opening fire in Victoria Park. As they pushed and shoved one another, someone tripped on the stairs leading to the ticket office. Around three hundred people were crushed on the stairwell resulting in 173 dead and 90 injured.

During the Spring of 1944, arrangements were made for men from northern Z batteries to go to London at weekends to give welcome and needed relief to their hard-pressed comrades. Among them were men of 101 (Sheffield) battery who provided crews for a battery sited in Southwark Park. (*Western Mail Archive*).

A parade to mark the fourth anniversary of the establishment of the Home Guard was held in Hyde Park. His Majesty King George VI takes the salute as the 3rd City of London battalion march past. 14 May 1944. (John Heddon. *Daily Mirror*).

The Home Guard stand down parade in London, December 1944. The scene at Piccadilly Circus. Stand down parades were held throughout the UK. (*Daily Mirror*).

Though the Home Guard did not officially admit women into its ranks, some units were willing to offer training to what became Britain's unofficial women's Home Guard. Dr Edith Summerskill, Labour MP for Fulham West and an active campaigner for equal rights, hounded the Secretary of State for War, and the War Office alike, urging official recognition and for the women to be fully integrated into the Home Guard.

By the beginning of March 1943, it was estimated there were around 25,000 women in more than 200 units. Many had received weapons training and were excellent shots, though they were realistic in their aims of being allowed to take over support roles such as clerks, telephone operators, wireless telegraphists, cooks, and first aid providers, thereby releasing men for combat duty.

With the Secretary of State for War expected to make a statement in Parliament, Miss G Courtney, secretary of the Mayfair section told the *Daily Mirror*.

"In the meantime, many of our ranks are getting tired of waiting for official recognition and are joining other women's services. It seems a waste of time for them to change when they are already banded together in organised groups. We have been promised that attention will be drawn to the matter, but it is still under consideration."

The outcome was that the women were given support roles though their only uniform was a broach. Summerskill and Dame Helen Gwynne-Vaughan continued to campaign for full recognition and the issuing of proper uniforms. They did however secure a letter of thanks for the women's contribution from King George VI on the standing down of the Home Guard in 1944. (*Mirrorpix*).

Mrs. W C Thiele (right) and Mrs. P Bartlett of the Upper Thames River Patrol (Home Guard) at Maidenhead. January 1941. (*Mirrorpix*)

Industry Goes to War

As early as 1935, the Government had developed its scheme for shadow factories in the event of war. Though it was a dispersal scheme to reduce the risk from bombing, a shadow factory was not a secret location but a duplicate of the original as to how it was equipped and staffed. Initially, emphasis was given to creating shadow factories for engine production, especially the Rolls-Royce Merlin and the Bristol Hercules, though Bristol would only allow components to be manufactured rather than complete engines.

Beyond these were dispersal factories, some of which changed production. Axminster Carpets at Axminster, Devon, turned to making stirrup pumps. Terry's Chocolate in York was taken over by Hills & Son, Stockton on Tees, to manufacture propellor blades. At Newcastle-under-Lyme, Staffordshire, BSA built a factory on farmland to manufacture 20mm Hispano cannons. There were also decoy factories deliberately intended to attract the attentions of the Luftwaffe.

The Government opened training centres so the unemployed could learn some of the skills needed for working in the munitions industry, and the war was only two weeks old when the plan was announced for the gradual drafting at least one million women into war work. The women would replace men released for service in the armed forces. The plan envisaged they would replace men in occupations such as bus conductors, railway cleaners, textile workers, clerks, shop assistants, and in processed food factories. At this early stage of the war, it was thought that at least 500,000 women would be needed by munitions works, though not in skilled work.

Between September 1940 and the end of 1941, the armed forces and Civil Defence proposed to increase their establishments by a total of 1,750,000 men and 84,000 women, a course of action that would require 500,000 workers giving up their jobs.

Just a few of an estimated 8000 men attending Government Training Centres in December 1940. There were fourteen centres at the start of the war, rising to a maximum of 38 before being reduced to twenty in 1943.

Over the same period, the munitions industries were looking to recruit an additional 1,500,000 people. It was proposed that women could be recruited to fill as many unskilled or semi-skilled jobs as possible and single woman in the 19-24 age group were called up. By the end of 1941, the scheme had been extended to include women up to the age of 30 and would eventually be extended to include women aged 18-51. Once registered, a person was invited for an interview at their local Labour Exchange, and, if not already in a job considered essential to the war effort, they would be asked to consider taking up work of national importance. Those refusing could be compelled.

Firms of all shapes and sizes would become involved in the war effort, from the small workshop off Boathouse Lane, Stockton, that produced the strips of aluminium foil dropped by our bombers to confuse enemy radar, to the purpose-built Castle Bromwich Spitfire Factory

On 22 October 1939, the Ford Motor Co was asked to locate, equip, and manage a shadow factory for the mass production of Rolls-Royce Merlin XX aero engines. Ford's expertise at mass production was urgently required, though it was also vitally important that aero engine components should be fully interchangeable regardless of manufacturer. Initially, part of the old Ford factory at Trafford Park, Manchester, was turned into a tool room, and machine tools, technicians and draughtsmen were transferred from Dagenham. Rolls-Royce provided drawings and seconded skilled engineers. By September 1940, several buildings had been erected at Eccles and 2300 workers hired.

As most skilled workers in the UK were already employed, Ford had to rely on untrained men, youths, and women. Even so, the first production Merlins were delivered to aircraft manufacturers during June 1941. In March 1942, Eccles was asked to increase production from 400 to 600 engines a month and by April 1944 the workforce of 17,307, including 5828 women, were turning out 900 engines a month as well as a steady supply of spare parts. Mass production at Eccles brought the book price of a Merlin down from £5640 to £2484 each.

On 20 March 1940, the government announced that steel was to be rationed from 1 April. All Government Departments as well as industry would be affected by the scheme. It was designed to dovetail into the licensing system then operating in order that supplies of steel would be equitably distributed. One of the first effects was the reduction in steel allocated to the production of private cars.

On 14 May 1940, Winston Churchill appointed the Canadian-British Max Aitken, 1st Baron Beaverbrook, as Minister of Aircraft Production (MAP). Beaverbrook, or Max Aitken has he was then, entered Parliament at the general election of December 1910 when he was elected the Liberal Unionist member for Ashton-under-Lyne. Ennobled in January 1917, he served out the last few months of the Great War as Chancellor of the Duchy of Lancaster and Minister of Information.

In November 1916, he acquired the controlling interest in the *Daily Express*, though it remained a secret until late 1918. Under his leadership, the Express was transformed within twenty years from a poor imitation of the *Daily Mail* selling 350,000 copies a day, to the country's top daily with a circulation of 2,329,000 copies.

Beaverbrook brought those same organizational skills into play at MAP. Trevor Westbrook of Vickers Armstrong (Aviation) Ltd was brought on board. Others who joined the ministry, Horace Clarke who worked in the development of alloys. He became Director of Light Alloys (Aluminium and Magnesium). George Usher who was later appointed Controller General of Materials Production. Francis Banks an aero-engine fuels specialist who had been in charge of fuel for Britain's entrants in the Schneider Trophy races, was put in charge of aero-engine production, and A H Hird, on secondment from Vickers-Armstrong held sway at the Machine Tools Directorate.

Beset by industrial relations so abysmal that workers were threatening strike action, poor management skills, and an indifference to using tooling and drawings supplied by Supermarine that defied logic, the incomplete shadow factory at Castle Bromwich had yet to complete a single Spitfire, despite promising sixty a week from the beginning of April. The plant was supposedly being run by the Nuffield Organisation. Only three days after taking office, Beaverbrook effectively conned Lord Nuffield into placing the plant under ministry control.

Incensed at being out-manoeuvred, Nuffield complained to Churchill. Unfortunately for Nuffield, Beaverbrook sent in Sir Charles Fairey of Fairey Aviation who compiled a damning report on the place.

Beaverbrook brought in managers from Supermarine and handed the factory over to Vickers Armstrong (Aircraft). Beaverbrook met with Air Chief Marshall Hugh Dowding and both were convinced that, in the short term, the RAF was going to need fighter aircraft rather than bombers. Castle Bromwich's bomber contracts were immediately cancelled, and priority given to building Spitfires. Ten Mk II Spitfires were completed during June 1940, twenty-three in July, just under forty in August and nearly sixty during September.

Though Hurricane and Spitfire fighter production had priority, they formed part of Beaverbrook's 'Five Types' project, the others being three

bombers - the Bristol Blenheim, the Avro Wellington and the Armstrong Whitworth Whitley. Output of other types of aircraft were scaled back as materials were redirected.

Almost immediately upon taking office, Beaverbrook cancelled deliveries of all training aircraft from the United States to the UK, insisting that valuable space on merchant ships be given to bringing over fighter aircraft.

Writing for the *London Gazette* (page 4545) in September 1946, Dowding summed up Beaverbrook's appointment. "The effect of this appointment can be described as magical, and thereafter the supply situation improved to such a degree that the heavy aircraft wastage which was later incurred during the Battle of Britain ceased to be a primary danger, its place being taken by the difficulty of producing trained fighter pilots in adequate numbers."

An American fighter plane is reassembled straight from its packing crate. During the first year of the war, 743 aircraft were delivered from the USA, though many were North American Harvard training aircraft. The picture might have been taken at the Fairey Aviation shadow factory at Burton Wood which specialised in the assembly of aircraft imported from the USA. (*Mirrorpix*).

The ministry reorganised aircraft repairs by establishing the Civilian Repair Organisation (CRO). Fighter aircraft with light damage that could be rectified within a few hours were to return to base for repair by RAF personnel. Those with damage likely to take around twenty-four hours to rectify, but still flyable, were directed to land at improvised repair depots established about thirty miles west of London. The pilot would wait for the repairs to be completed then fly the aircraft back to base. Those too shot up to fly to a repair depot were moved by road. Badly damaged aircraft were sent for rebuilding or to be stripped of anything and everything that could be reused.

Civilian Repair Units (CRU) were set up, often at civil airfields, though part of the LMS Locomotive Works at Derby became a CRU dedicated to repairing Hurricane wings.

Some CRUs specialized in salvaging repairable components from crash sites. The system allowed even quite small businesses to play vital roles in returning aircraft to the front line. By the end of the war, the CRO had repaired and returned to service 82,000 aircraft and 167,000 aero engines.

In recent years, claims have been made that aircraft production was increasing regardless of Beaverbrook's role. In 1939 the UK produced 7940 aircraft for the Services. Nearly double that number were produced during 1940 with 15,049 aircraft, and in 1941 production passed 20,000 for the first time. By the end of the war, the Services were receiving 2500 new aircraft of all types every month.

On 5 March 1941, the Essential Work Order became law. Any establishment where work was considered essential to the war effort had to gain the consent from the Ministry of Labour National Service Officer prior to sacking an employee. Also, workers could not leave their employment without permission. The National Service Officer had powers to deal with those workers guilty of serious absenteeism.

By the end of 1941, more than 100,000 firms were on the Register of Protected Establishments whereby their essential and highly skilled employees were classed as working in reserved occupations and therefore not liable for military service, though they were still eligible for part-time duty with the Home Guard or on ARP.

CANTEEN SERVICE

The new CANTEEN will be OPEN MONDAY NEXT, SEPT. 29th. Those wishing to have Dinners on that day should purchase their tickets from the Canteen on Saturday Sept. 27th

The following prices will be Charged in the Canteen

Meat 2 Vegetables, Bread	10d & 11d
Fish ,, ,,	10d
Boiled Pudding & Cutard	3d
Milk ,, ,,	3d
Stewed Fruit ,,	3d
Cakes	1½d & 2d
Tea	per ½ pint 1d
Coffee or Cocoa	,, 1½d

Employees should note that they are expected to provide their own Knife, Fork & Spoon

(Page opposite). Former silk worker Mrs. D Robinson found wartime work as a tractor driver with the Bristol Aeroplane Company. She is pictured moving a 14-cylinder Hercules radial engine, one of 57,400 manufactured by the company during the war. Designed by Sir Roy Fedden, the Hercules went into full production during 1939 with the introduction of the 1290hp (960kW) Hercules I. There were four major variants, culminating in the 1735hp (1294Kw) Hercules XVII.

Bristol developed the power-egg, a modular (unitised) Hercules where the complete engine and cowling were supplied as a single unit enabling quick engine changes. Aircraft fitted with Hercules engines included the Bristol Beaufighter, Armstrong Whitworth Albermarle, Vickers Wellington, Short Stirling, and Handley Page Halifax. (*Daily Mirror*).

Some of the ladies charged with providing more than 2400 hot meals a day at an aircraft factory canteen "Somewhere in the West of England." (*Bristol Evening World*).

Originally designed as a heavy fighter, the Bristol Beaufighter proved a successful rocket firing ground attack plane as well as a reliable torpedo bomber. Originally built by the Bristol Aircraft Company at Filton, two shadow factories were quickly brought into operation for final assembly. One was operated by Fairey Aviation at Stockport, the other by Bristol at Weston-super-Mare.
(*Official. Daily Mirror*)

Micrometres at the ready. An aircraft inspection department operating out of a pub. Between 15 and 26 September 1940, the Supermarine Spitfire factory at Southampton was attacked three times. The heavy damage inflicted upon buildings at Woolston during the last raid was so great that they were never rebuilt. In line with other aircraft manufacturers, Supermarine had dispersed some of its activities but the problems at the Castle Bromwich factory had hampered progress.

However, as Castle Bromwich was starting to turn out aircraft, Lord Beaverbrook ordered Supermarine to disperse to premises already identified as suitable. These included the Hants & Dorset Bus Depot in Winchester Road, Southampton, as well as many of the city's garages. Eventually, there were 64 dispersed sites. (*Daily Mirror*).

Plexi-domes for RAF bomber aircraft being manufactured at Eagle Components, Thames Ditton. (Bernard Alfieri Jnr, *Mirrorpix*).

Hawker employees Winnie Bennett, Dolly Bennett, Florence Simpson, and an unnamed colleague on the Hurricane fighter production line. When the war started, the RAF had eighteen Hurricane squadrons in service and the aircraft went on to account for 60 per cent of the Luftwaffe's losses during the Battle of Britain. In all, 14,487 Hurricanes were manufactured up to the end of production in July 1944. (Official, *Mirrorpix*).

Hawker Typhoon assembly at the Gloster Aircraft Co. The company had dispersed to 48 sites scattered mainly around Gloucester, Cheltenham, and Stroud, and at its height employed 14,000 workers. (*Northcliffe Newspapers*).

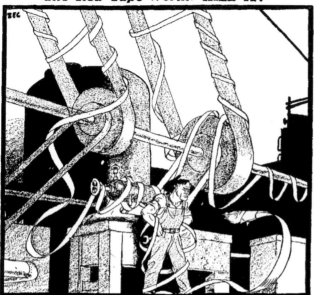

The Red Tape-Worm—KILL IT!

Philip Zec cartoon featuring Lord Beaverbrook taking on red tape. Published in the *Daily Mirror* on 1 July 1940, Zec drew the cartoon in response to a page one Muddle Campaign story. An aluminium works' employing 350 people and working round the clock seven days a week, producing aluminium for aircraft and other munitions. The works leading authority on the treatment of aluminium and on training unskilled labour to use it, had been drafted into the army where he was doing odd jobs around a Royal Artillery barracks. The firm believed his release from the army would enable the firm to increase production by a third in a matter of months. Repeated requests to the War Office had got nowhere as had an appeal to the Ministry of Supply. The firm was sending a full report to Lord Beaverbrook who had quickly gained a reputation for cutting through red tape. (Philip Zec. *Daily Mirror*).

The women's pilot section of the Air Transport Auxiliary. Despite many of them having more flying hours than most RAF pilots, these women had to fight prejudice to be accepted. They flew aircraft from factories to front line RAF squadrons. When they took off in a type they had not previously flown, they flew with the manual on their laps. When one of them delivered a Lancaster bomber to a base, the aircraft was searched because it was thought a woman could not handle such an aircraft. Left to right: Miss Pauline Gower (leader), Mrs Winifred Crossley, and Miss M Cunnison. (Official. *Westminster Press*).

Workers at a barrage balloon factory. Balloons were partially inflated to allow the seams to be checked for leaks. When fully inflated, each balloon held around 19,000 cubic feet of highly flammable hydrogen gas and measured 63 feet x 31 feet. It could take around forty minutes to raise a balloon to operational height of around 6000 feet (1829 metres). (*Mirrorpix*).

The Dunlop Rubber Co. barrage balloon factory at Gaythorn gasworks, Manchester. The gasworks had ceased production and has been relegated to a distribution point in 1929 when a new facility opened at Partington. (Official. *Mirrorpix*).

Nuffield Mechanizations Ltd, Drens Lane, Ward End, Birmingham, building Crusader heavy cruiser tanks. Originally Wolseley Motors, the company had been bought from the receivers by William Morris (later Lord Nuffield) in 1927 for £730,000 (£46.2 million in 2019) as a private investment. The Nuffield-designed Crusader, was almost six tons heavier than other British cruiser tanks of the period and required five road wheels to distribute its weight of nearly 20 tons. (*Birmingham Post & Mail*).

A Crusader tank on test on Salisbury Plain. The MkI and MkII variants carried a 2 pounder (40mm) gun as main armament; the MkIII carried a 6 pounder (57mm). Other Crusader designs included anti-aircraft, gun tractor, and armoured recovery vehicle variants. Powered by a Nuffield Liberty 27-litre V-12 petrol engine, the Crusader had a top speed of 26mph (42kmh) on roads and 15mph (24kmh) off road. In all 5300 were built between 1940-43. (*Mirrorpix*).

(Below). It was not until June 1941 that this type of tank was designated the Matilda II. So, when this image was taken in November 1940, it was simply described as a light tank, though the official designation was the type A12. It is seen here trundling into Derby Market Place during a parade marking the town's War Weapons Week.

The Matilda II went into production during 1938 when 140 were ordered from the locomotive manufacturers Vulcan Foundry, Newton-le-Willows. Powered by a pair of AEC C1 water-cooled diesel engines, the 25 ton tank had a top speed of 16mph (26kmh) on roads and 9mph (14kmh) off road. Its armour included a 78mm (3.07inch) thick frontal glacis and 75mm protection all around the turret. It carried a quick-firing 2 pounder (40mm) that fired anti-tank rounds. To the right of this was a Vickers water-cooled .303 machine gun (7.92mm). The tank pictured here is what was then known as a MkIIA, and this type carried a BESA 7.92mm in place of the Vickers.

As construction included some difficult castings, orders were placed with heavy engineering and railway workshops including Ruston & Hornsby at Lincoln; John Fowler & Co at Leeds; the LMS locomotive works at Horwich; the Harland & Wolff shipyard in Belfast, and the North British Locomotive Co in Glasgow. (*Derby Telegraph*).

Cooking the Nazi goose!

Philip Zec cartoon of 16 July 1940, following Lord Beaverbrook's appeal for the women of Britain to give up their aluminium pots and pans so they can be turned into Hurricanes, Spitfires, Blenheims and Wellingtons. (Philip Zec. *Daily Mirror*).

WAAFs give a hand loading hundreds of thousands of salvaged aluminium milk bottle tops at the Midland County Dairy yard, Birmingham. It was estimated that only 50 per cent of Birmingham's milk bottle tops were being salvaged, and the photograph was part of the drive to increase it. March 1943. (Below). Old prams at a scrap yard in Edinburgh, await recycling into aircraft parts. May 1940. (*Mirrorpix*).

Nothing remained sacred when it came to salvage for the war effort. Iron railings are removed from the cemetery in Jesmond, Newcastle upon Tyne, September 1942. Then again, nothing remained sacred when it came to salvaging the salvage. Writing in the *Daily Mirror* for 10 September 1942, Helen MacGregor reported how items put out for the local salvage steward to collect sometimes disappeared. White rags were 'recycled' to the local First Aid Post. Pieces of velvet or soft wool spirited away to be made into cuddly toys for children in factory workers' cretches. Tea caddies purloined to keep fertilizer or insecticide in as the wartime containers they were supplied in were prone to leaking. (*Mirrorpix*).

WWI German howitzer on its way to being recycled for the war effort. (*Mirrorpix*).

Workers Playtime? Well not quite. This balancing act was just one of the cunning plans employed by workers to persuade the old tramlines around Hull to lift off the track bed. The rails, made from high grade steel, were destined for recycling for use in the munitions industries. (*Mirrorpix*).

Your kitchen range must burn less this winter !

Get to know it better. Persuade it to do more — for less! Every scuttle saved means more for the factories, to swell the output of weapons — to finish the job.

ECONOMISE IN EVERY WAY YOU CAN

Here are some examples :

Have a fire in one room only—breakfast in the kitchen	Wrap up hot water pipes and tanks to retain heat
Never use your oven for a single dish	Waste occurs when dampers are open unnecessarily
Use less hot water for baths and washing up	Sift and use all cinders, and use coal dust for banking

Call at your Coal Office or Gas or Electricity Showroom for advice and leaflets on how to economise.

Save FUEL for the factories

All Fuels are equally important

COAL · COKE · GAS · ELECTRICITY · FUEL OIL · PARAFFIN

A BAN ON ALL FORMS OF HEATING

AN APPEAL

to every man & woman in the Country

CENTRAL HEATING in all Public Premises, Offices, Shops, blocks of Flats, etc., has been prohibited until the Autumn, by Government Order. Restrictions have also been imposed on the use of all other methods of heating such premises. These measures have been dictated by the urgent need to save Fuel for essential war purposes.

Play *your* part at home
DO NOT USE YOUR
COAL, GAS or ELECTRIC FIRES
FROM NOW ON

Remember, gas and electricity come from coal. Illness must be the only reason for lighting a fire before the autumn.

We must SAVE FUEL for Battle

The LMS fuel economy exhibition coach. The less gas, coal, electric and water the householder used, the more there was for industry. "Only five inches of hot water in your bath…..more hot water for Hitler."

Shell cases in production at a factory in South Wales. When these images were cleared for publication on 18 March 1940, many of the 1100 workers had only recently become involved in munitions work. (Below). The picture shows metal being poured into ingots. After the rough edges have been sheared off, the ingots went to a furnace for reheating prior to hot rolling. Rolling removed surface impurities and eventually resulted in a bar five feet long, twelve inches wide and three quarters of an inch thick.

Test firings of shells were carried out at the Royal Artillery Proving Range, Salthouse Point. At low tide the rounds were recovered from the mudflats for examination. (*Swansea Evening Post*).

(Below). The contribution made to the war effort by Britain's steel industry was enormous and in certain areas critical. For the first eighteen months of the war, the Vickers Works at Sheffield had the only 15-ton drop-hammer in the country capable of forming the crankshaft for the Rolls-Royce Merlin engine. So vital was this machine to the country's very survival, it was worked sixteen hours a day, seven days a week. Had it been put out of action during the summer of 1940, the effectiveness of RAF Fighter Command would have been seriously undermined.

Around Sheffield there were at least two hundred steelmaking firms came in all shapes and sizes, from small specialist craft workshops to vast complexes employing thousands of workers. Some firms such as the International Twist Drill Co. continued as normal, producing twist drills, reamers, milling cutters and machine tooling. However, demand rocketed and the company opened new factories at Brough, Huddersfield, and Bradford. By 1945, International's output was at least 600 per cent above that of 1939.

Others were switched to part munitions, part normal production. Edgar Allen & Co. continued to manufacture parts for railway locomotives, hydraulic machinery, machine tools, and equipment used in quarries and cement works. They produced 10,000 tons of quality munitions castings including 872 Matilda and 515 Churchill tank turrets as well as 116,743 components for tanks. They also produced enough manganese steel sheet to manufacture 1,115,600 helmets and enough bullet core sheets to make 28,114,016 bullets.

At Steel, Peach & Tozer's Ickles Works around 50 per cent of wartime production consisted of gun forgings ranging from 2 pounder (40mm) anti-tank to 6 inch (152.4mm) naval guns. The English Steel Corporation's main output was armour plate, springs and components for tanks, side and deck armour for warships, bomb casings, and more than half of the country's output of forgings for the 17 pounder (76.2mm) anti-tank gun.

Designed by Barnes Wallis, who at the time was working for Vickers Armstrong, the RAF's 12,000 pound (5443 kg) Tall Boy and the 22,000 pound (9979 kg) Grand Slam bombs were cast at English Steel, Sheffield. The production of the Grand Slam necessitated a departure from the usual method of making castings of that size, and special arrangements had to be made for machining them.

Ingot capacity for aluminium rose from 31,000 tons in 1939 to 55,000 tons in 1943. When salvaged and imports were added, aluminium production during 1943 was 300,000 tons. (*Newcastle Chronicle & Journal*).

Output from steel works rocketed. During the war, Firth Brown & Co, Sheffield, produced more than 1 million tons of high-quality alloy steels. The tonnage would have been even higher had not the Luftwaffe blown the roof off the melting shop during the Blitz, forcing the furnaces to be shut down for lack of night time cover.

(Below). Tending to the furnaces as production continues round the clock. Steel production was controlled by the Ministry of Supply, with annual output of around 13 million tons. It dropped to 11.8 million tons in 1945. (*Newcastle Chronicle & Journal*).

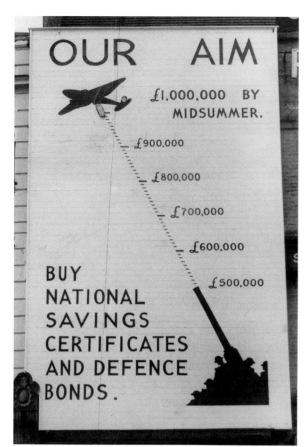

OUR AIM

£1,000,000 BY MIDSUMMER.

£900,000
£800,000
£700,000
£600,000
£500,000

BUY NATIONAL SAVINGS CERTIFICATES AND DEFENCE BONDS.

On 22 August 1940, the pointer for midsummer was the £1million (£56.4 million in 2019) mark on the target indicator at the National Savings Office in Derby Market Place. (*Derby Telegraph*).

(Below) War Weapons Week at Rhondda. The first tranche of war weapons weeks ran between 16 September 1940 and 28 June 1941. The total raised, including what was termed 'small savings,' amounted to £469,007,713, (£23,854,450,442 in 2019). (*Western Mail*).

(Opposite page top). War Weapons Week at Newport, Monmouthshire, during February 1942. A second tranche of War Weapons Weeks were held between 18 October 1941 and 28 March 1942, raising a total of £545,640,770 (£25,902,019,204 in 2019). (*Western Mail*).

(Opposite page bottom). The Wings for Victory campaign ran from 6 March to 3 July 1943, though towns were free to decide when to take part. Nationwide, the campaign raised £615,945,713 (£28,296,247,879 in 2019). This image was taken during Manchester's campaign. 23 March 1943. (George Greenwell, *Daily Mirror*).

Two images from Derby depicting the registration of 40-year-old men and 50-year-old women at the Derby Employment Exchange. In March 1941, Minister of Labour, Ernest Bevin, brought in the Essential Work Order, requiring all women aged 18-60 to register for work. Women who were pregnant, or had children under the age of 14 living with them, could not be forced to do war work though they could volunteer. Women whose husbands were either in the armed forces, or living at home, were directed into work that could be anywhere in the country. (*Derby Telegraph*).

Winston Churchill on a visit to the Cammell Laird shipyard, Birkenhead, on 26 April 1941. Also in the picture are Laird's chairman and managing director, Robert S Johnson, and the Chief Constable, Captain A C Dawson. Though managing director for twenty years, Johnson had recently been appointed chairman following the death of Lionel Hichens in an air raid on London. Hichens had been chairman for thirty years and had steered the company back from the brink of collapse during the Depression.

In the 1930s, Lairds built HMS *Ark Royal*, the first warship in the world to be designed from the keel upwards as an aircraft carrier. During the war, the yard completed 106 naval vessels of all types including the battleship HMS *Prince of Wales*, as well as repairing and refitting many more. The yard also undertook repairs and refits to 2000 merchant ships.

Lairds is thought to have had one of the most expensive civilian air raid shelters ever to be constructed in the UK during the war. Located 80 feet below ground level, the shelter could accommodate 6000 people and was equipped with a canteen, surgery, toilets, and possibly a library. It was built during 1940 at a cost of £129,000 (£7.28 million in 2019). (*Liverpool Echo*).

Women riveters at work in a Scottish shipyard. This image was published on page 5 of the Wednesday 4 March 1942 edition of the *Daily Mirror*. (*Mirrorpix*).

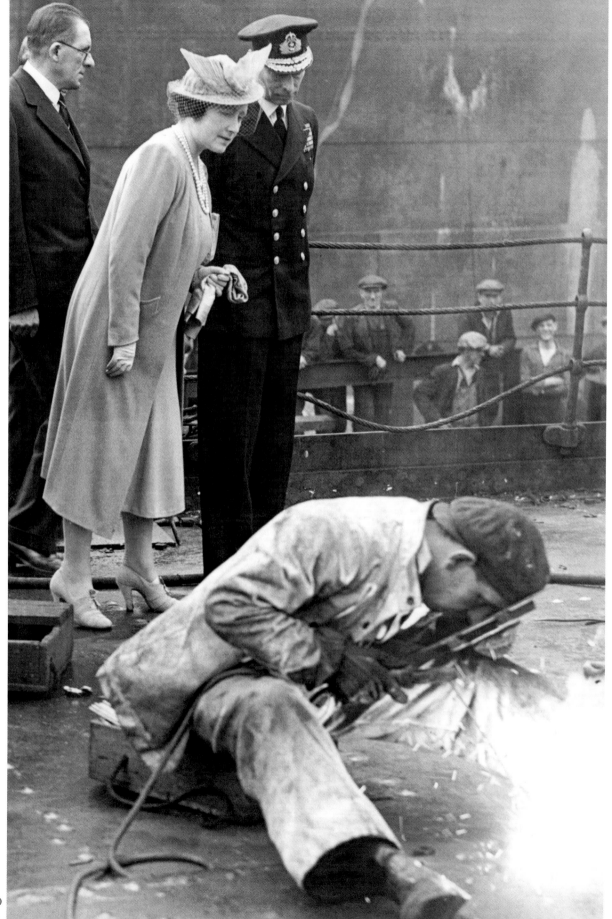

There were several royal visits to north east shipyards. (Opposite page). King George VI and Queen Elizabeth watch a welder in action during their visit to Tyneside in June 1941. (This page). King George VI and Queen Elizabeth at John Readhead, South Shields, 9 April 1943. (*Newcastle Chronicle & Journal*).

Shortly before midnight on 13 December 1942, the 8316grt Norwegian-owned tanker *Vardefjell* broke in two during heavy weather whilst taking part in convoy KMS 5 from the Clyde to North Africa. The front section floated off taking with it all the senior deck officers. The aft section also remained afloat with 31 crew members on board including all the engineers.

Sometime later, the two sections were close enough to one another for the men on the aft section to attempt a rescue and two lifeboats were launched. However, the weather was so bad that both lifeboats were destroyed, and chief engineer Rolf Ugelstad and stoker John Opheim were lost. The last sighting of the forepart was around 0700hrs on 14 December, after which it presumably sank, taking ten crew members including her skipper, Captain Nils A Ambjornsen, with it.

The 29 survivors on the still afloat aft section elected the boatswain, Einar Halvorsen, to take charge, though he was helped by the second engineer Anders Skotheim. With the bulkhead holding, but unable to steer, the aft section headed stern first in the general direction of the UK. Four days later, they were spotted by a British aircraft and, on the 20th, two aircraft spent a couple of hours circling before they dropped red smoke bombs and left. On the 22nd, a Sunderland flying boat attempted to contact them by Morse lamp but no one on board could understand what it meant.

Land sighted on Christmas Eve turned out not to be Ireland or the UK but Vaag on the Faroe Islands. The survivors were taken off, though the second engineer returned later hoping to take the aft section to sheltered waters. However, the weather was too rough, and the attempt abandoned. From surviving accounts, it took the engineers several attempts to bring their wayward charge, still loaded with 3000 tons of oil, under control.

Eventually, the aft section was towed to Kirkwall and later to Methil on the east coast of Scotland. From there it was towed to the Tyne, arriving on 5 March 1943.

The decision was taken to repair her. A new front section was ordered from the shipyard of Sir James Laing, Sunderland, and was launched on 27 March 1944. After fitting out, the new section was towed to the Tyne and is seen here in the care of the Readhead & Dry paddle tugs *Malta* and *Conqueror*. The repaired *Vardefjell* sailed from the Tyne on her trials on 18 July 1944, joining convoy ON246 Liverpool to New York seven days later. (*Mirrorpix*).

It was early evening on Saturday, 23 October 1943, when five motor gunboats (MGBs) slipped their moorings and proceeded along the Humber and out into the North Sea. Once clear of the coastal minefield they altered course for the Skagerrak and increased speed. The first mission of *Operation Bridford* was on.

Even before the outbreak of war, British industry had relied on Sweden for ball-bearings, machine tools and some specialist steels and, by July 1940, it was apparent that Britain's war effort would be seriously undermined if supplies could not be maintained.

The man charged with maintaining supplies was 40-year-old metallurgist-cum-Arctic explorer Frederick George Binney, who in 1939 had been despatched to Sweden by the Ministry of Supply (Iron & Steel Control). Binney was also a commander in the Royal Naval Reserve and well-connected with the twilight worlds of military and naval intelligence as well as the Ministry of Economic Warfare.

On 23 January 1941, Binney organised the break-out of five Norwegian merchant ships interned in Swedish ports with around 25,000 tonnes of highly desirable machine tools, ball-bearings, special steels, ingots, and engineering equipment sitting in their holds. The operation was a complete success though not without danger as the ships narrowly missed the German battlecruisers *Scharnhorst* and *Gneisenau*.

For political purposes it was decided the MGBs would fly the red ensign of the merchant navy and be crewed by merchant seamen. The boats would be based at Hull (where around 80 per cent of their crews lived) and managed by Ellerman Wilson Lines. They were gutted, enabling each of them to carry about 45 tons of cargo at a maximum speed of 28 knots. Binney chose their names. *Hopewell*, *Nonsuch*, *Gay Viking*, *Gay Corsair* and *Master Standfast*.

The basic operation was to run the German blockade of the Skagerrak during the hours of darkness. Upon entering Swedish waters, they would head for Lysekil, load, and make the return run at night so that by daybreak they would be well into the North Sea with air cover supplied by the RAF.

On the first run, only the *Gay Viking* reached Sweden. The MGB was experiencing engine trouble and had been left behind as the four other boats pressed on. However, during the 27th, repeated sightings of German aircraft led Binney to believe the operation had been compromised so he ordered his four boats to return to Hull. In the meantime, blissfully unaware of unfolding events, *Gay Viking* was again under way at best possible speed, entering Swedish waters at 0400 hrs and arriving at *Lysekil* shortly after 0700hrs. After loading, she slipped out on the evening of 29 October, arriving at Immingham on the morning of 31st.

By the summer of 1944, Binney's Navy had successfully brought more than 340 tonnes of desperately needed ball-bearings and engineering equipment to the UK, but the short summer nights curtailed operations. When winter returned, the blockade runners were again at sea, though now they were involved in covert operations for the SOE. On 6 February 1945, the *Gay Viking*, *Hopewell* and *Nonsuch* took part in Operation Moonshine delivering small arms and ammunition to the Dutch resistance, during which *Gay Viking* sank after being in collision with *Hopewell*. Our image shows *Gay Viking* (Captain H Whitfield) in July 1944. (Official, *Mirrorpix*).

Getting the workers to work. Ellen McShane at work on the Jarrow on Tyne ferry, May 1942. (*Mirrorpix*).

Some of the first women to be recruited as gangers at work on the LNER at Sheffield. (*Daily Mirror*).

FOREMAN'S GOOD DEED

Helps Worker's Indigestion

Dear Sirs.   Staffs.

After suffering for years with a Gastric Stomach, I went off my eating.

The Foreman at the Works told me about MACLEAN BRAND Stomach Powder and advised me to give it a trial.

Then my wife said "*Why don't you try MACLEAN BRAND Stomach Powder.*" So I sent for a bottle.

After the first dose all pains gone, I commenced to eat four meals a day. From 8-st. 6-lbs. I gained up to 10-st. 8-lbs.

People at the Works where I work said since I have gained my health back "*You don't look like the same man, as you look a picture of health.*"   (Sgd.) G.T.

The wide popularity of MACLEAN BRAND Stomach Powder is convincing evidence of the efficacy of this speedy and successful remedy for Pain, Flatulence, Heartburn, Nausea and proved safeguard against Gastritis and Stomach Ulcer.

MACLEAN BRAND Stomach Powder is only genuine if the signature ALEX.C.MACLEAN appears on the package.

MACLEAN Brand Stomach Powder

Price 2/3.

Also in Tablet Form in 7d. boxes, or bottles at 1/5 and 2/3 (including Purchase Tax).

Mrs Irene Pack was one of hundreds of women who qualified to work in railway signal boxes. Initially, the LMS trained women to take over relatively unskilled roles, but as the war progressed selected women were trained as passenger guards, signalmen, electricians, fitters, boiler cleaners, blacksmiths, and painters, though they were not trained for footplate duties. About 17 per cent of the LMS workforce were women. (*Mirrorpix*).

At the outbreak of war, 744,000 men were employed in the coal-mining industry, even though 61per cent of coal was being cut by machine. However, by June 1941 the figure had dropped alarmingly forcing the Minister of Labour and National Service, Ernest Bevin, to issue a 'standstill' order preventing miners from being called up for military service. Bevin also broadcast an appeal for former miners to return to the pits.

Bevin announced that instead of being conscripted into the armed forces, one in ten young men would be chosen by ballot and sent to the mines. It did not go down well. Apprentices in Clydeside shipyards were among those who came out on strike. They were willing to go into the forces, but to remove them from apprenticeships designed to turn them into skilled workers and put them to unskilled work in a pit was barking mad.

Bevin Boys were soon demanding more pay or subsistence allowances. During January 1944, things were coming to a head. The Ministry of Labour ruled out subsistence allowances as it would open the flood gates to demands from other workers who had been directed into jobs away from home. As to pay, a Bevin Boy aged 19 was paid £2. 8s (£2.40p) a week (approx. £107.73 in 2019). At the time, a London contingent of Bevin Boys at Haunchwood Colliery – none of whom wanted to be down a pit though they were more than willing to join the armed forces - were demanding an extra £2. 4s a week and were prepared to go on strike even if it meant each of them facing three months in jail or a £100 (£4648 in 2019) fine.

Bevin Boys at Holmeside & South Moor Collieries' Morrison Old Pit, Annefield Plain. Initial training consisted of four weeks classroom-based work at a training centre, followed by two weeks at their assigned colliery working alongside an experienced miner. The majority of Bevin Boys were not employed cutting coal. Conscientious objectors could volunteer for mine work under a separate scheme. (*Newcastle Chronicle & Journal*).

Owned by the Butterley Co, Ollerton Colliery was one of five pits sunk during the 1920s to exploit coal reserves in mid-Nottinghamshire. In 1939, the UK produced 231 million tons of coal, yet despite the urgency of war, production steadily declined to 183 million tons in 1945. There were many reasons. The loss of skilled miners to the armed forces, poor industrial relations, shortages of timber, steel, coal-cutting machinery and conveyor machinery were just a few of them. (Below). Striking miners at Nine Mile Point Colliery, Cwmfelinfach, draw their last full week's pay, March 1944. In October 1935, the colliery was the scene of the first ever 'stay down strike' in the South Wales Coalfield, over the mine owners' use of 'scab labour,' that is men not members of a mineworkers Federation. The 164 strikers remained underground for 177 hours, coming up when the owners agreed they would employ only Federation men. (*Mirrorpix*).

In mid-August 1940, the Government banned the manufacture of hosiery, which it classed as "luxury trade." On 21 October, Nottingham's largest firm of silk throwsters, Windley & Co, closed with the immediate loss of 400 jobs. The Government insisted that only Government contracts could be worked on and Windley's did not have any. What they did have was enough silk to manufacture 2.5 million pairs of stockings. Along with other manufacturers, they sought permission to release 1.5 million pairs of stockings for the Christmas 1940 market. They were refused and ordered to export them, only they did not have an export market. (*Mirrorpix*).

A salute from King George VI to cheering workers at the conclusion of a royal visit to Spode Copeland, Stoke-on-Trent, in February 1941. The king and queen also visited Shelton Steelworks. The royal couple were on a nationwide tour to boost morale.

In March 1940, the 1500 workers at the Royal Doulton Pottery, Burslem, found a notice at the gates. "This factory has so many orders for export markets that it is necessary in the country's interests that work should proceed throughout Easter week-end, with the exception of Monday, March 25, when the factory will be closed." (*Stoke Sentinel*).

Sixteen-year-old Vera May Stone blowing laboratory glassware at Prestons, West Street, Sheffield, in June 1942. This was highly specialized, Vera having to precisely control the shape and dimensions of each piece. (*Daily Mirror*).

Dating from 1552, Ye Olde Wellington Inn next to the market square in the Shambles, was one of the oldest buildings in central Manchester. Somehow this half-timbered masterpiece survived the raid. This image was taken on 23 December and banned from publication. (*Mirrorpix*).

The Blitz

The Blitz is defined as the period of the heavy bombing of British cities from 7 September 1940 until mid-May 1941 when Luftwaffe units were withdrawn to prepare for the invasion of Russia. The Blitz was a final attempt to finish Britain off following Germany's failure to win either of their Kanalkampf (Channel War) and Battle of Britain campaigns. It too would be a strategic failure.

During the period we now call the Phoney War, the Luftwaffe carried out many 'tip and run' raids, often by single aircraft testing our defences or unloading unused bombs from combat patrols. However, the first bomb to be dropped on Britain was at just before 8.00am on 24 September 1939, when a house at Headlington near Oxford suffered a direct hit from a practice bomb accidently released by a RAF aircraft. The bomb failed to detonate but, even so, a young evacuee was seriously injured.

The first attack by the Luftwaffe on mainland Britain was carried out on Monday, 16 October, when nine Junkers JU88s bombed warships in the Firth of Forth. The cruisers HMS Edinburgh and Southampton, along with the destroyer HMS Mohawk, were damaged.

Following the fall of Norway, Teesside was awarded the honour of being the first industrialised area of the UK to be targeted when bombs were dropped on Cargo Fleet, Southbank, and Grangetown. No air raid warning was given, and little damage done.

On the night of 19/20 June, Hull recorded its first raid though only minor damage was caused and there were no casualties. A week later during the early hours of the 27th, Swansea was raided, and bombs were dropped on the Danygraig area though again there were no reported casualties. That same day, a lone raider attacked Middlesbrough. One bomb smashed through the deck of the suspended car of the Transporter Bridge putting it out of action for a few hours. St Peter's Church and vicarage were wrecked. The vicar was out on ARP duty, and his wife and daughter who would normally have taken shelter in the vicarage cellar were away on holiday.

The public conveniences at Town Hall corner took a direct hit and cottages in Wood Street and School Croft were wrecked beyond repair.

The first major attack on Tyneside took place in the late afternoon of 2 July 1940. Considerable damage was done around Jarrow and Newcastle when a bomber thought to be targeting the Tyne High Level Bridge hit the Spillers' factory. Thirteen people were killed and 123 injured. Commencing on 3 July, Cardiff was bombed three times in nine days and then again on 7 August.

On 4 July, the Kanalkampf (Channel War) opened with attacks on coastal towns, ports and shipping though it was not until six days later that a large force of bombers (26 aircraft) concentrated on a single target, a west-bound convoy. They were escorted by nearly fifty fighters that became embroiled in a dogfight with thirty Hurricanes sent to intercept. Of the 150 bombs dropped, only one scored a direct hit.

On 16 July, Hitler issued Fuhrer Directive 16, setting in motion planning for an invasion of Britain. For the plan to succeed, four criteria had to be met. The reduction of the RAF to a level where it could no longer defend the country. The Channel to be swept of British mines and the invasion route protected on either side by newly laid minefields. Royal Navy warships in home waters to be put out of action. Royal Navy warships elsewhere, such as the Mediterranean Fleet, kept occupied so they could not steam to the rescue.

The head of the Luftwaffe, Reichsmarschall Herman Goering, told Hitler that given four clear days the RAF could be destroyed. On 31 July, convinced that victory was assured, Hitler authorised an all-out attack and preliminary raids were made against south coast ports and the coast-long chain radar network. The airfields of the RAF's 11 Group, responsible for defending the south east and the capital, came under attack in what was now a war of attrition, though RAF Manston was the only airfield ever to be out of action for more than twenty-four hours. In the first five days, the Luftwaffe lost 251 aircraft, the RAF 118. It was not one-sided. The RAF Blenheims took the battle to the Luftwaffe, constantly raiding their airfields in France.

On the night of 28 August, the country's main west coast port, Liverpool, was raided by a force of 160 bombers. They returned for the following three nights and, by the end of the year, the city had been attacked fifty times.

The Luftwaffe seriously underestimated RAF fighter strength and the RAF seriously overestimated Luftwaffe strength. It was a simple mistake due to both sides being unsure as to how many aircraft constituted a squadron. An RAF fighter squadron was usually twenty aircraft. In the Luftwaffe the fighter strength of a staffel was twelve aircraft. Fighter Command's aim was for each squadron to have at least twelve aircraft operational at any given time and double that number of pilots.

By the second week of August, the Luftwaffe had lost 181 bombers and 105 Bf109 fighters. The RAF had lost 148 aircraft, though more important for them was the loss of trained pilots. During July, 84 pilots, or ten per cent of the Fighter Command establishment, had been lost. During August, it was 237, and in September a further 264 made the ultimate sacrifice. It is worth noting that throughout this period the British aircraft industry

was working around the clock, turning out 200 more aircraft than the German factories which, to maintain the myth of Nazi invincibility, were still working under normal peace-time conditions.

With losses mounting and no sign of the RAF collapsing, the decision was taken to switch to bombing Britain's industrial areas. The decision was driven by the fact that the Luftwaffe had sustained serious losses - by 7 September it was 721 aircraft. Switching to night bombing ought to offer some protection from the RAF and the devastation and demoralising effect of such raids must surely bring the British to their senses.

Saturday 7 September 1940, and the weather was clear. At 4.00pm the coast-long chain radar detected a large enemy force heading toward the UK. The RAF was no longer the primary target, and Observer Corps posts were soon verifying a new objective – London. Every available fighter 11 Group could muster was scrambled, and they needed to be as the bombers had friends with them in the shape of 600 fighters.

The concentration point for the 318 bombers was London's docklands. By the time the raiders left,

Birmingham AFS put their canal firefloat through its paces. (*Birmingham Post & Mail*).

warehouses had been transformed into infernos and the residential areas of Wapping, Bow, Silver Town, West Ham and Bermondsey had suffered heavy damage. At 8.00pm the raiders returned. By the time the all-clear sounded at 5.00am, nine miles of waterfront was ablaze and 448 people had been killed. London would be bombed for the next 56 consecutive nights. The Blitz had begun.

Now celebrated as Battle of Britain Day, the action fought on 15 September finally broke the back of the Luftwaffe's daylight offensive and was to lead to the postponement of the invasion of Britain. It was mid-morning when Winston Churchill paid a visit to 11 Group headquarters. All was unusually quiet. "The bastards are up to something." And so they were. Soon the radar chain had picked up 250+ German aircraft on their way and more were following.

The attackers faced a strong headwind so their fighter escort was forced to fly even slower than usual using up valuable fuel. It gave 11 Group time to put new tactics into play - its fighter squadrons were to form up in pairs and attack together. To the north at 12 Group's RAF Duxford there was time for all five squadrons based there to take off, form up into a big wing and head for the enemy. Having overestimated losses, Luftwaffe pilots had been told the RAF was close to breaking point and were somewhat surprised when pounced upon by 160 Hurricanes and Spitfires.

Mid-November saw the implementation of the Luftwaffe's change in tactics by extending the Night Blitz to the provinces. On the night of the 14th, Coventry was raided by 552 aircraft in an attack that lasted eleven hours. Fires quickly took hold, and, as they flew over the Channel, crews of some of the later aircraft mistook a faint red glow in the sky for what they thought might be some sort of night fighter beacon. It was Coventry burning. On the ground, the glow could be seen from as far away as Birmingham, Rugby, and Derby.

In Coventry, chaos reigned. The Civil Defence Control Centre had taken a direct hit and local communications now relied almost entirely upon the undoubted bravery of teenagers and boy scouts who made their way through mayhem relaying messages to police, fire crews, first aid parties and rescue squads.

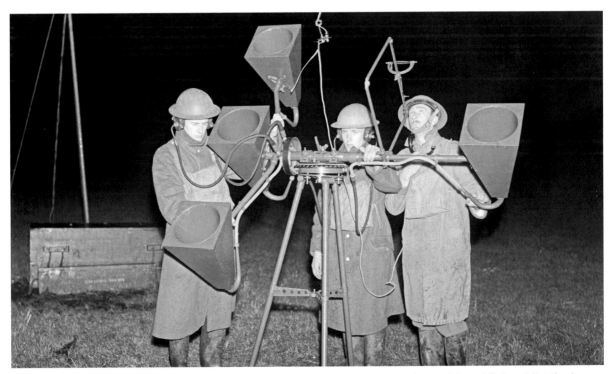

Aircraft noise sound locator attached to a searchlight unit. Locators were given wide publicity whilst the home chain radar system remained highly secret. (*Birmingham Post & Mail*).

Adding to Coventry's problems was the fact that all roads in and out were blocked with debris and the railway line severely damaged. Help was on its way from surrounding towns as well as a convoy from the London Fire Brigade. It would be hours before any would get through.

So devastating was the raid that the government lifted reporting restrictions and allowed the target to be named. The image of a city where one third of its centre, including its cathedral, had been destroyed completely went round the world and aroused strong feelings against Nazi Germany. A new word entered the lexicon of warfare – Coventration – the destruction of a city by aerial bombardment. What was not reported was that the local authorities almost lost control of the situation and troops called in to clear the rubble were also there to maintain order.

One of the lessons learned from Coventry was the need for crash evacuations - a system whereby those made homeless in a blitz-type raid could be evacuated quickly and effectively instead of being left to their own devices. One of the first cities to establish a crash evacuation plan was Hull, though by January 1941, Hull was preparing a more

detailed scheme organised by their Director of Education, R C Moore.

Before the end of November, Bristol, Liverpool, Southampton and Birmingham had been subjected to heavy raids. During December, weather conditions were such that the Luftwaffe were grounded. However, they still mounted eleven major and five moderately heavy raids. London suffered three major and twelve light raids.

At 7.00pm on the night of 12 December 1940, the sirens wailed their ominous 'Raiders Approaching' warning across Sheffield. Within minutes, many citizens would have heard the distinctive double beat of the non-synchronized engines as the first of the German bombers approached - answered by the rip-rip sound of the defending anti-aircraft batteries.

The Luftwaffe codenamed the attack 'Schmelziefel' (Crucible), assigning 406 aircraft to the destruction of much of Britain's iron and steel industry. By the time the raid ended at around 3am the following morning, 336 bombers had reported in over Sheffield, dropping a total of 355 tonnes of HE and 16,452 incendiaries.

Observer Corps "Raiders overhead." (*Daily Mirror*).

Though the Luftwaffe's concentration point for the raid was the industrial area to the north east, the city centre was extensively damaged. The heaviest loss of life in a single incident was at the Marples Hotel. Situated at the junction of High Street and Fitzalan Square, the seven storey-high hotel received a direct hit from a high explosive bomb at 11.44pm, and collapsed in flames into its unstrengthened main cellar, where it is thought around seventy-five people were sheltering.

Rescue work was under way by about 10am the following morning and, surprisingly, several survivors were pulled from the debris of the hotel's bottling store. They had managed to shelter under a part of the store's ceiling that had held. The rescue work was to drag on for some weeks and involved clearing around 1000 tons of rubble. In all, sixty-four bodies were recovered together with parts of six or seven others. Only fourteen of the victims could be positively named, others were identified from personal belongings.

Before the month was out, Birmingham, Manchester, Liverpool, Portsmouth, and Leicester had also been attacked. Things were not going entirely the Luftwaffe's way. Between the beginning of October and the end of December, they lost 384 bombers of which 140 could be attributed to enemy action. The remainder were lost through non-combatant causes such as bad landings on inadequately equipped airfields or training accidents.

In Washington, USA, the British Government received a note from the German Embassy offering to suspend all air raids for the Christmas period provided Britain reciprocated. The unofficial truce lasted from Christmas Eve, through Christmas Day, and resumed at 6.45pm on Boxing Day with a raid by 108 aircraft on London, though it appears this was retaliation for raids carried out by the RAF on Luftwaffe bases.

Also, during December 1940, the Press and Censorship Bureau introduced a new procedure, blocking the release of images featuring damage to well-known locations. The '28-day & 2nd Raid rule,' was intended to deny the Luftwaffe Intelligence Section information useful in compiling reports on the effectiveness of specific raids.

A Royal Observer Corps Centre where all aircraft, friendly and enemy alike, were plotted. Observer posts were in direct contact with their local centre, and the centres were in direct contact with RAF Fighter Command. (Official. *Mirrorpix*).

On the night of Saturday 11 January 1941, London was once again the target. Bank station took a direct hit, the bomb detonating in the booking hall. The blast wave was funnelled down the escalator causing the roof to collapse and blowing passengers into the path of an oncoming train. Though the train's automatic brake engaged, it was too late for some of the people in its path. A rescue party from Liverpool Street station arrived and within three hours the dead and injured had been taken away. To get road traffic moving, a temporary bridge was thrown across what soon became known as 'the largest crater in London.' The bridge was officially opened by the Lord Mayor on 3 February. By May, the roadway had been repaired and the bridge removed.

On the eve of the German invasion of Russia, the combat strength of the Luftwaffe stood at 4882 aircraft of which 1511 were bombers – 200 fewer than in May 1940. With more than half the bomber force committed to this new campaign, attacks on Britain continued though there were fewer large-scale raids. Some were termed nuisance raids, such as the one against Derby on Monday 27 July 1942.

It was a cold drizzly day with low cloud, and although there had been an alert at 6.00am, the all-clear had been sounded an hour later. At 7.50am, a lone aircraft skimmed the roof tops of the Rolls-Royce plant. It was so low it had to bank round the factory's water tower. A bomb was dropped on Royce's central stores, another destroyed No.4 gate and the houses opposite. The roof of No.4 Shop collapsed after being hit by a blast wave. The plane then turned and strafed Osmaston Road and the surrounding streets before making off towards the Friargate area, shooting down the Babington Lane barrage balloon along the way. A bus in Slack Lane was machine-gunned, though the intended target might well have been the LNER locomotive shed at Friargate station. In all, twenty-three people were killed.

On Christmas Eve 1941, an extraordinary raid took place that scared the living daylights out of thousands of Mancunians. At around 3.00pm, as hordes of people were out and about on Market Street doing some last-minute shopping, three bombers suddenly appeared with their bomb doors open.

Nearly two weeks before the Blitz began, Liverpool had been bombed several times, including a heavy raid by 160 bombers. (*Liverpool Echo*).

There had been no warning. People scattered, bowling one another over in the panic to find shelter. However, panic turned to anger when it was discovered that the bombers were dropping 10,000 road safety leaflets from the Chief Constable of Manchester, John Maxwell. This was not the first leaflet raid on Manchester. On 8 August 1940, a German bomber dropped a bundle that unfortunately failed to open. Its fall was broken by a police officer guarding the entrance to the Civil Defence Report & Control Centre, Salford. It landed on his head.

By January 1942, the Luftwaffe front-line units were so desperate for crews that training was cut by one month. The following month the quartermaster general's office stated it was no longer able to forecast the availability of new aircraft or spares as rates of production could not keep up with losses.

In March 1942, the RAF bombed the historic town of Lubeck, and the Luftwaffe retaliated with what became known as the Baedeker Blitz; raids on British towns and cities noted for their cultural heritage.

It is said the Luftwaffe used the detailed maps in Baedeker Guides for targeting purposes. The raids, caried out during April and May, were assigned to Luftflotte 3 and included their elite pathfinder squadron KGr100. Attacks would be carried out by 30-40 aircraft and each target was to be raided on two consecutive nights.

The first Baedeker raid, against Exeter on 23/24 April, resulted in 200 houses being damaged. Five people were killed, and eight injured. The following night the attack came in two waves each of twenty aircraft, many returning to reload and come back a second time. There was widespread damage and 73 people killed with 54 injured. The raids on Exeter cost the Luftwaffe five aircraft.

Bath was in the firing line for the nights of 25/26 and 26/27, resulting in 400 casualties and widespread damage. The raids on Norwich and York resulted in 67 and 79 killed respectively, and 43 people died when Canterbury was attacked. Baedeker raids continued ad hoc for the remainder of 1942.

Damage to the assembly hall at the High School for Girls, Wallasey, after a bomb came through the roof. September 1940. (*Liverpool Echo*).

During 1942-43, there were less than thirty raids on London, though 1944 opened with the Little Blitz. The Luftwaffe had managed to assemble a hotchpotch of 550 aircraft in northern France but, as many of the crews were untrained, a pathfinder unit had to be employed. On 21 January, a two-wave attack totalling 447 aircraft failed mainly due to poor navigation and only 32 tonnes of bombs fell on the capital. By May 1944, the Luftwaffe in France had just 144 operational aircraft available for raids.

At 3.50am on 13 June 1944, the sirens warned of an impending attack. Anti-aircraft batteries opened fire on a single aircraft that crashed a few minutes later on open land at Barking. About thirty minutes after that a second plane crashed but this time it came down in a populated area causing casualties. It was two or three days before the authorities realised that the Luftwaffe had deployed a new weapon - the V1, a rocket powered, pilotless flying bomb armed with a 1000kg warhead. The weapon was equipped with an autopilot and when the fuel ran out, the distinctive sound made by its engine stopped and it plummeted to earth and exploded. The Germans calculated how much fuel a V1 would need to reach its intended target area, aim it in the general direction and launch. By the end of June 660, V1s had hit London; others had come down in the Portsmouth/Southampton area.

The Germans instructed their agents, including Eddie Chapman, to monitor where the V1s landed and report the location and damage caused. Only thing was that Eddie was a double agent as were the other German agents sending back information. By carefully coordinating their messages, they convinced German intelligence that damage caused by V1s landing around north west London were given times of V1s landing in south east London. The idea was to convince the Germans they were overshooting. They would then adjust fuel levels and the V1s would fall short of much of the capital. To lend credibility to Chapman's reports, he was allowed to send photographs of real damage caused by V1s to Germany via Lisbon. Chapman was the only Englishman ever to be awarded the Iron Cross by Adolf Hitler.

As the frequency of this type of attack increased, it was decided to move the anti-aircraft batteries to the coast where, by sheer weight of firepower, they destroyed more than half of all incoming V1s. Fighter aircraft also intercepted incoming V1s, pilots closing then using a wing to flip the weapons off course.

By the end of August, the British Second Army had overrun the V1 launch sites in the Pas-de-Calais, forcing the Germans to adopt the practice of air-launching the weapons from Heinkel III bombers. More than 700 were launched by this method, though many exploded upon release taking their mothership with them. Others were launched at targets further afield including Manchester and Oldham, where 27 people died in one explosion.

On 8 September, a mysterious explosion destroyed parts of Chiswick and Epping. The first V2 had landed. The V2 was a 14 tonne, 45 foot (13.7 metre) long rocket launched from a mobile platform. It travelled at supersonic speed which meant it landed and exploded before anyone heard it arrive. It flew too high and too fast for any RAF fighter to intercept it or anti-aircraft battery to shoot it down. In all, 518 V2s landed on London, killing 2274 people, and seriously injuring 6000 others. The last V2 landed on 25 March 1945 at Orpington. A few hours later, the last V1 came down. It fell on Chislehurst.

The last raid occurred on the night of 17/18 March 1945, when the Luftwaffe sortied 18 aircraft. Eleven of them crossed the east coast between Scarborough and Walton-on-the-Naze to attack Hull, resulting in twelve people killed and 22 seriously injured. The total civilian casualties from raids and V weapon attacks were 60,595 killed and 86,182 seriously injured.

The main heavy anti-aircraft guns were the 3.7 inch (94mm) which entered quantity production from 1938 onwards and the 4.5 inch (114.3mm) which is pictured here. A 3.7 inch Mk III gun with a No.1 predictor had a range between 23,500 (7200 metres) feet and 24,600 (7500 metres) feet depending on the fuse setting. The 4.5 inch could be fired at the maximum rate of twelve rounds per gun per minute. The shells weighed 55 pounds (24.9Kg) with a maximum range of 41,000ft (12,500m), well above the ceiling of any known bomber. This image is of a Northern Command gun, possibly sited at Hedon for the defence of Hull. By July 1940, London could boast 92 modern heavy anti-aircraft guns. Newcastle also had 92; Birmingham 67; Liverpool 64; Derby 48; Portsmouth 44; Southampton 43; Edinburgh 40; Glasgow and Clydeside 27; Plymouth 22; Nottingham 21; Manchester 20, and Cardiff 12. The port of Swansea had just three heavy guns, though more were added. (*Hull Daily Mail*).

(Below). American troops man a 40 mm light anti-aircraft Bofors gun at Plymouth. 1944. (*Mirrorpix*).

Barrage balloon and winch lorry. Balloons held around 19,000 cubic feet (538 cubic metres) of highly flammable hydrogen gas. By July 1940, London was defended by a barrage of more than 300 balloons. (*Official. Westminster Press*).

(Top right). Barrage balloons also took to the water, providing docks and shipyards with a little extra protection such as discouraging minelaying aircraft. Also, they were an integral part of towns' barrage defences as they completed the encirclement. The balloons were flown from barges, each of which had a designated mooring point from where its balloon would be deployed. Each balloon barge was manned by a RAF detachment of eight men and a sergeant. (*Newcastle Chronicle & Journal*)

In January 1941, Balloon Command were asked to consider a suggestion that the flying of balloons could be undertaken by WAAFs. It was hard work, the balloons had to be manned twenty-four hours a day and were often flown in the most appalling weather conditions.

There had been some technical improvements to equipment, including the mechanization of some aspects of handling but Balloon Command still thought the job required physical strength not usually possessed by women. However, it was decided to have a trial run.

Thus, on a cold, wet, morning in April 1941, twenty WAAF volunteers attended their first course at Cardington. By the end of June, they had proved their worth and the Sheffield barrage was chosen as the site for a full-scale experiment. In July, the women took over D Flight of 939 Squadron and by the end of the year all balloons, except for those on isolated sites, had been handed over to the WAAF.

Thousands of WAAF officers, NCOs and air women were transferred to Balloon Command, releasing their male colleagues for front line service. Balloon Command went on a recruitment drive. It was open to healthy women of a minimum height of 5ft 1in (1.55metres) and up to 43 years-of-age. The minimum pay was three shillings (15p) a day, all found. Any married woman who enlisted and whose husband was in the services continued to receive her allowances and was to be granted leave to coincide with that of her husband, subject to service conditions.

At first, the substitution of WAAFs for airmen on balloon sites was not as straightforward as it might appear. Even though technical improvements in balloon handling meant that physical strength was no longer a prime consideration, it still took sixteen WAAFs to replace ten men. Also, RAF balloon crews were integrated into military defence schemes whereas the WAAFs were non-combatants. (*Manchester Evening News*).

Londoners leave their bombed-out home with whatever they could salvage, including the all-important wireless set. Passed by the censor. 9 September 1940. (*Daily Mirror*).

Titled the "FLAG POST," this image was taken in London's East End two days after the raid of 7 September 1940. It was passed by the censor for immediate publication. (*Daily Mirror*).

(Below). By the end of September 1940, London's underground stations were providing nightly shelter for 177,000 people. However, tube stations were not as safe as people imagined. On 17 September, the blast wave from a direct hit on Marble Arch station ripped tiles off the walls turning them into shrapnel. Twenty people were killed. There would be more tube casualties before the end of the year. (*Newcastle Chronicle & Journal*).

(Opposite page). Dated 9 September 1940. A London double decker bus leans against 34 Harrington Square Garden, North London, having been hurled there by the blast wave from an exploding bomb. (George Greenwell, *Daily Mirror*).

The morning of 15 November found the Queen's Hotel, Hertford Street, Coventry, still ablaze. The decision was taken to blow up the building to prevent fire spreading to the Post Office. It might have been far worse. Throughout the night, raiders had arrived overhead to drop their bombs and incendiaries. Had all 552 aircraft passed over the city within half an hour, the conditions might well have been created for a firestorm. As it was, the fires quickly spread, especially around the cathedral where there were many half-timbered buildings, narrow winding alleyways, and courtyards. (*Birmingham Post & Mail*).

(Below). The blitzed and still smouldering ruin of Coventry Cathedral. (*Daily Mirror*).

Remains of a Corporation bus near the burned-out Owen Owen department store. The people of Coventry regarded the Owen Owen conflagration as the city's second most 'famous' fire of the raid, the cathedral being the first. (*Birmingham Post & Mail*).

(Below). With many of Coventry's food shops out of action, one alternative source for obtaining rationed items was this lorry parked at the Midland Red Bus Station, Meadow Pool. (*Coventry Evening Telegraph*).

People gather around a Ministry of Information van parked outside the Hippodrome Theatre, Coventry. The man at the microphone is Godfrey Baseley, who would go on to become the originator of the BBC Radio series *The Archers*. Baseley's role was to go from one blitzed town to another advising people how to obtain replacement ration books and clothing, pass on information regarding evacuations, and how to contact the local authority regarding repairs to houses.

One of the scams following a raid was for people to present themselves to the local authorities claiming to have been bombed-out. They would then be issued with a new identification card and ration book. One man managed to pull the stunt nineteen times before he was caught. (*Coventry Evening Telegraph*).

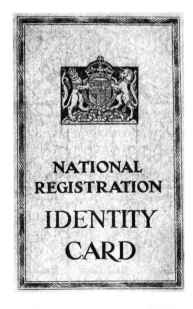

The first mass funeral for those killed in Coventry Blitz was held at the city's London Road Cemetery on Wednesday 20 November, with the burial of 172 victims. At the time, bodies were still being dug out of the rubble and a second mass funeral for a further 250 victims took place the following Saturday. These were the first mass burials of Blitz victims in the UK. The cost was borne by the Government. One advantage was it spared relatives the harrowing ordeal of attempting to identify loved ones. (*Mirrorpix*).

Following the raid on Coventry, a second round of evacuations from industrial towns began. Here children from Birmingham arrive at Ripley station, Derbyshire. 15 November 1940. (*Derby Telegraph*).

The Birmingham Blitz lasted from 9 August 1940, when a single bomb fell on Erdington, to 23 April 1943, when two bombs fell on Bordesley Green. However, between these dates the city would suffer more than its fair share of heavy raids. The first major raid occurred on the night of Tuesday 19 November, when 357 long-range bombers dropped 403 tonnes of HE bombs, including 48 parachute mines, and 29,160 incendiaries. At least three fires were still burning when the raiders returned the following night dropping 132.3 tonnes of HE and 9472 incendiaries.

The night of 21/22 November bought some respite due to continuous rain, low cloud, and poor visibility. Birmingham was not so lucky on the night of 22/23 when a drawn-out raid lasting eleven hours saw 227 tonnes of HE and 16,452 incendiaries dropped. The main concern was the direct hit on Bristol Road South that destroyed three gravity-fed water mains leaving 60 per cent of the city without water. This forced fire crews to fight what fires they could from wherever they could find water. Royal Engineers were deployed with orders that should the raiders come again they were free to blast fire breaks should the need arise. No building was off limits for destruction.

(Top). October 1940. A small crowd of onlookers watch workmen filling in a bomb crater outside Greys, Bull Street. As the raid began, several buses unloaded their passengers outside the store though, after about an hour, the driver of the No.9 decided to make a run for it, loaded his passengers and set off. Minutes later the bomb hit. (*Birmingham Post & Mail*).

(Middle) The devastation at the corner of John Bright Street and Hill Street was caused by a land mine. The curved structure at right background is the roof of New Street station. (*Daily Mirror*).

(Bottom). Corporation bus caught in a bomb blast at Sparkbrook. 20 November 1940. (*Birmingham Post & Mail*).

Bristol suffered its first major raid of the war on the night of 24 November 1940, when 134 bombers of Luftflotte 3 dropped 160 tonnes of HE, 11,578 incendiaries, and 938 explosive incendiaries in an attack lasting from 6.30 till 11.00pm. Much of the city centre was destroyed though the docks escaped comparatively lightly. Luftwaffe aircrew reported seeing whole blocks on fire and one explosion (possibly a gas holder) that produced a sheet of flames at least 400 metres high. Casualties were put at 200 killed, 163 seriously injured and 526 slightly injured.

On the night of Friday 3 January 1941, the city was attacked by 178 bombers in two waves commencing at 6.35 pm. After a lull of just over an hour, the second wave arrived at 12.40 am, the all-clear sounding at 5.51 am. The damage was extensive and a granary at the City Docks containing 8000 tons of grain was destroyed. Twenty tramcars were destroyed when the Bedminster Depot, West Street, was hit.

On Good Friday 11 April, Bristol suffered its last major attack of the war, the area around the docks including Queen Square, Canon's Marsh and Prince Street taking a pounding. The raid also marked the end of Bristol's tramway system. The city council could have saved their money as Luftwaffe did the closing down for them by scoring a direct hit on St Phillip's Bridge. Not only was the bridge destroyed but also the tramway's main power cable which ran across it.

It is said that after the raid, the last serviceable tram made it back to the depot through the combined efforts of being pushed by the conductor assisted by passers-by, then freewheeling where the gradient allowed it.

(Right) Originally built in the Netherlands in 1676 and later dismantled and brought to Bristol, the Old Dutch House was a casualty of the 24/25 November raid. It was subsequently demolished. (*Daily Mirror*). (Below) Bridge Street, Bristol. 24 November 1940. (*Bristol Post*).

Dolphin Street looking towards Union Street, Bristol. 25 November 1940. (*Bristol Post*).

Bristol's tramway system was already in decline before the outbreak of war. The city council wanted rid and had paid £1,125,000 (approximately £74 million in 2019) to acquire it with the sole intention of ripping it up. The Luftwaffe did the job for them. This image was not released for publication until 26 April 1941. (Simon Galloway, *Bristol Post*).

Sheffield's turn came on the night of 12 December 1940, when the city was raided by 336 bombers dropping 355 tonnes of HE and 16,452 incendiaries. At 10.35 pm, aircrews in the area reported seeing a tremendous explosion presumed to be a gasworks going up. Sheffield's anti-aircraft guns fired 3700 rounds. Our image shows fire engulfing the High Street department store of John Walsh. (*Mirrorpix*).
(Below). Sheffield AFS in action. (*Daily Mirror*).

High Street, Sheffield, on the morning of 13 December 1940. In the background, a wall at what remains of the C&A Modes store, leans precariously inwards. Other stores wrecked included Robert Brothers, Crossley's, Campbell's furniture, and T B & W Cockayne. The King's Head Hotel (dating back to 1572) and the Angel Hotel (where a celebration dinner marking Wellington's victory at Waterloo was taking place) were destroyed.

The city was still clearing the rubble when the Luftwaffe returned on the 15th, dropping 80 tonnes of HE and 21,600 incendiaries. (Below) King George VI and Queen Elizabeth meet with people bombed out of their homes during the raids on Sheffield. (*Daily Mirror*).

In what later became known as the Christmas Blitz, Manchester was raided on 22/23 and 23/24 December 1940. Within minutes of the sirens sounding on the evening of the 22nd, incendiaries were dropping on and around Albert Square as Luftflotte 3 pathfinder unit KGr 100 dropped nearly 10,000 incendiaries. Less than two hours into the raid, part of the massive Victoria Building collapsed into Deansgate and ARP reinforcements from Salford were stopped dead when a building at the corner of Bridge Street and Gartside Street collapsed blocking the road. Along Portland Street, Sackville Street and Watson Street, fires rampaged through warehouses and a stick of HE bombs ripped Gray Street, Stafford Street and Cooke Street apart. There were lucky escapes. Around 450 people were trapped by debris in Gibson's shelter in Erskine Street but thankfully all were saved. The destruction was on an unprecedented scale, the likes of which Manchester had never experienced. To make matters worse, 200 firefighters and their equipment were still at Liverpool where they had been sent the previous evening. Forty minutes after the last of Luftflotte 3's 149 bombers had turned for home, the first of 121 aircraft of Luftflotte 2 began their bombing runs. In all 272 tonnes of HE and 37,152 incendiaries were dropped.

The following evening, Luftflotte 3 paid a return visit. The attack was again led by pathfinder unit KGr100 who dropped more than 9000 incendiaries in a little over fifty minutes. However, it was the eighteen aircraft of 1/KG28 that packed the surprise punch. Each aircraft carried two LM1000 parachute mines, the Luftwaffe's heaviest bombs.

At about 3.00am Christmas Eve morning, the fires were contained even if many were burning furiously. Additional firefighting reinforcements had arrived including forty pumps and seven hose lorries from the LFB. It was then that fate played its hand. A strong wind blew up carrying sparks and embers far and wide over the badly mauled Piccadilly area reigniting some fires and starting fresh ones. Soon a wall of fire, that had to be seen to be believed, extended from Moseley Street across the length of Piccadilly to Portland Street and beyond. As it was threatening to engulf Princes Street, there was little alternative other than calling in the Royal Engineers to blast fire breaks.

(Above). Fire crews tackling the blaze at the devastated warehouse at the junction of Parker Street and Portland Street, Piccadilly. There were so many fires, the MFB was forced to make on-the-spot decisions as which to fight and which to leave. Some decisions were made for them as collapsing buildings made roads impassable to fire appliances and manhandled trailer pumps alike. (*Mirrorpix*).

The early hours of Monday 23 December 1940 - and fires at Manchester Exchange railway station are out of control. The station was severely damaged, and part of the main roof collapsed. All lines through the station were blocked though, by New Year's Day, limited operations had been restored with one platform in either direction available for use. On 8 January, all platforms were reopened for limited use. The station was not fully operational until 19 May 1941. Initially banned from publication by the Censor. (*Manchester Evening News*). (Below). Cannon Street, Manchester on the morning of 24 December. This picture was banned from publication. (Thompson, *Daily Mirror*).

An LM1000 parachute mine that failed to detonate when dropped on Manchester on the night of 23/24 December 1940. Having a high explosive to weight ratio, these mines caused considerable damage in built-up areas. The skin of the 8ft 8inch (2.64metres) long device was too thin to allow it to free fall, hence the parachute. On release from the bomber, the rear cone housing the parachute was pulled clear by means of a wire attached to the fuselage of the aircraft, thereby allowing the parachute to deploy.

The weapon was fitted with a clockwork fuse, activated on impact, and timed to detonate twenty-five seconds after arming. The tail cone of the mine pictured here is still partially intact. Because parachute mines were primarily a naval weapon, responsibility for defusing them was with the Royal Navy. (*Manchester Evening News*).

The 1kg incendiary bomb. The weapon that did the most damage weighed less than a bag of sugar. A He 111 bomber could carry 32 cannisters, each containing 36 incendiaries capable of creating a ribbon of fire nearly a mile in length. (*Mirrorpix*).

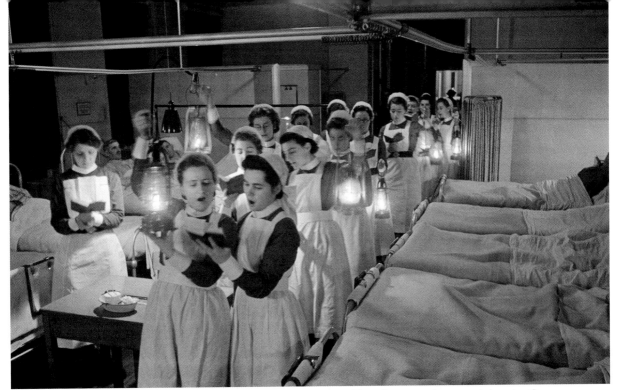

Nurses at Westminster Hospital visit the wards singing carols. The photographs were taken by George Greenwell on Christmas Eve and, for hospital staff and patients alike, it would be a night free from bombing. (George Greenwell, *Daily Mirror*).

Christmas 1940 and Santa pays a surprise visit to children sheltering in the tunnels of the London Underground. Published in the Sunday Pictorial on 22 December. (*Sunday Mirror*).

The attack, on Sunday 29 December 1940, was dubbed "The Second Fire of London," though it was also known as the "HE Fire Blitz." It began at 6.17pm when the lead aircraft of the Luftwaffe pathfinder unit KGr100r, approached at an altitude of 1000 metres to drop marker flares over the concentration point – the square mile of the City.

When the last of KGr100's ten He III aircraft flew over some thirty-three minutes later, its crew reported seeing seventeen large fires and 54 smaller ones. The raid lasted just 2hrs 13min, during which time 156 bombers dropped 127 tonnes of HE and 22,068 incendiaries. Many of the crews were able to bomb visually due to breaks in the cloud cover.

The reason the attack was concentrated in such a short time frame was the Luftwaffe's preference to get the aircraft safely on the ground again before poor weather came in. This is the scene that greeted *Daily Mirror* photographer George Greenwood when looking out from the dome of St Paul's Cathedral. The image was published across pages 6 and 7 of the Tuesday 31 December, edition. (*Daily Mirror*).

Two more of George Greenwell's superb images taken from St Paul's. One image is looking down at the towers of the West front, whilst, in the other, George is pointing his camera north-west. Paternoster Square is in the foreground. (*Daily Mirror*).

YOU CAN BE READY

Join now and train with your neighbours

AUXILIARY FIRE SERVICE
CIVIL DEFENCE CORPS
SPECIAL CONSTABULARY

CD
CIVIL DEFENCE

Fiction meets fact. Warden Percy Dale assisting a victim of the blitz. However, the image of Percy and his ward was one of a series of studio poses for use on Civil Defence recruitment posters. It carries a default file date of 1 October 1940, though it could have been taken earlier. On the other hand, the background is very real. It was taken by George Greenwell in Paternoster Row on the night of 29 December 1940. Though Percy's photograph is staged, it served a purpose as a much-needed morale booster.

The most famous morale booster photograph was taken by Fred Morley on 9 October 1940, depicting a milkman making his way through the rubble of a bombed London street to deliver his milk. With the Percy Dale image, the firefighters are real. However, Fred Morley's obliging milkman was in fact his assistant. (George Greenwell, *Daily Mirror*).

The scene in Paternoster Row on 29 December. (George Greenwell, *Daily Mirror*).

Searchlight in action on Clapham Common. (Tommy Lea. *Daily Mirror*).

146

This image, taken during the fire blitz, was published in the *Daily Mirror* on Tuesday, 31 December 1940. Interestingly, it has two captions, the original headed Gallant London Fire Service reads:

"During the recent air raid incendiary bombs fell in London causing some fires which were soon extinguished by the splendid work of London's firemen.

"(Picture shows) An explosive incendiary bomb exploding harmlessly in the roadway."

However, the raid had stretched the fire services to their very limit and on Monday 30 December, the Minister of Home Security, Herbert Morrison, quickly convened a meeting with the head of the London Fire Brigade, Commander A. N.G. Firebrace and senior ARP officers. The chief topic was incendiaries and how to deal with them. Their conclusion would be important enough for the minister to go on BBC radio and the Daily Mirror to rewrite the caption, using a cropped version of the image as part of the paper's lead story trailering Morrison's nationwide broadcast for volunteers.

The new caption read:

"Thousands upon thousands of incendiary bombs were rained on London during the fire blitz. Here are two burning in a city street. Incendiaries can be extinguished easily when they fall."

Morrison's broadcast was a call for more fire watchers. At the meeting, Commander Firebrace had told Morrison that the LFB had been fully committed fighting fires and they had had no time to search rooftops after each shower of incendiaries. The ARP representative for Bermondsey told Morrison, "We must have more watchers. If we get at the incendiaries quickly, we can stop most of the damage. Where there are no watchers it is often too late."

It was already law that all buildings where more than thirty people worked had to have fire watchers on the roof. The Courts were taking the matter seriously and those who broke the regulation were already being fined around £20 (£1128 in 2019) per offence, though the LFB and ARP authorities wanted tougher sanctions.

FIRE GUARDS get ready!
FIREBOMB FRITZ is coming

Men and women of Britain's Fire Guard *will* be ready. Ready because during quiet times we train and practise, every day learning to do our job better. We're not asking for trouble, but we'll meet it properly when it does come.

BRITAIN SHALL NOT BURN!

ISSUED BY THE MINISTRY OF HOME SECURITY

Within days of Herbert Morrison's broadcast appealing for people to volunteer for fire watching, rooftops around the country were manned. Here, a fire-watch team on a rooftop on City Road, Newcastle upon Tyne, await the raiders. January 1941. (*Newcastle Chronicle & Journal*).

On Saturday, 11 January 1941, Luftflotte 3 again raided London. The 137 bombers that reported over target dropped 144 tonnes of HE and 21,528 incendiaries. Liverpool Street and Bank stations were hit, killing 43 and 35 people, respectively. The images were taken by George Greenwell in Tabernacle Street. Interestingly, that two firefighters are holding the hose (branch) indicates that the water was being pumped through at around 100psi; a technique designed to 'knock out' a fire. The image inspired a painting by George Campbell that appears on the dust jacket of *The Blitz, Then and Now, Volume 2*. (*Daily Mirror*).

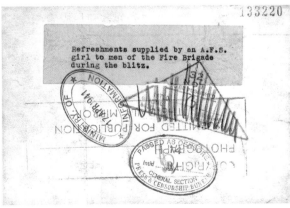

133220

Refreshments supplied by an A.F.S. girl to men of the Fire Brigade during the blitz.

Life goes on as normal for the three hundred families who had taken up permanent residence in the Ramsgate tunnels following an air raid in which 1200 houses were either destroyed or rendered unfit for human habitation. It is thought that just under 1000 people took up residence, quickly followed by subterranean greengrocers, a canteen, a barber's, and a hospital.

During the late 1930s, the mayor of Ramsgate applied to the Home Office for funds to excavate additional tunnels for use as air raid shelters and though it took three attempts to squeeze money out of the bureaucrats, the first new ARP tunnel was ready by June 1939. It was officially opened by the Duke of Kent. (*Mirrorpix*).

Up to the night of 13 March 1941, the shipbuilding town of Clydebank had pretty much escaped the attention of the Luftwaffe. Many lived in the town's 12,000 tenements and, to make matters worse, 90 per cent of the children evacuated in September 1939 were now back at home. The Nazis attacked on two successive nights and the results were devastating. Of the housing stock, only seven remained undamaged and 35,000 people were left homeless. People relied on mobile canteens for food, and water was brought in in barrels from Glasgow. Schools and halls were thrown open so that people had somewhere to sleep.

More than a third of the housing stock had either been destroyed or was subsequently demolished. More than 800 workers were drafted in to repair what remained, the work taking eighteen months to complete.
The following night, many people had taken to the nearby hills before the bombers struck. (*Daily Mirror*).

On Saturday 3 May 1941, the Luftwaffe launched a major attack against Liverpool and Birkenhead, dropping 363 tonnes of HE and 49,706 incendiaries. Though the main target was the docks and warehouses on the east bank of the Mersey, damage was widespread with 406 people killed in Liverpool, 57 in Bootle and sixteen in Litherland.

At 12.44 am, Luftwaffe crews in the target area reported a massive explosion and a sheet of flame rising 500 metres (1600 feet) into the air. As the last of the raiders turned for home at 3.40 am (double British summer time) they reported what appeared to be a continuous fire about six kilometres in length in the docks on the east bank. (*Daily Mirror*).

The shell of Lewis's Department store looking from the Adelphi Hotel. (Official. *Mirrorpix*).

Attempts to salvage the tangled remains of the Brocklebank cargo liner *Malakand* from what was left of Huskisson No.2 Dock, Liverpool, are under way. Despite valiant attempts to save her, the liner, laden with ammunition, blew up on the morning of 4 May scattering debris across a wide area. During the raid, the *Elstree Grange* and the *Europa* were sunk. (*Liverpool Echo*).

The scene outside Bush House, Aldwych, London, following a hit by a V1 flying bomb on 30 June 1944. At the time, Bush House was home to the BBC's Empire and European radio services, employing at least 1400 people. Interestingly, the show Shipmates Ahoy was going out live and listeners heard the V1 denotate as it landed.

It was here, in January 1941, that Victor de Laveleye, director of the Belgian service suggested opening broadcasts to Belgium with the Morse code dot, dot, dot, dash sound for the letter V – in this case meaning V for Victory. By happy coincidence, the opening of Beethoven's Fifth Symphony sounds similar. It was soon taken up by all the language services.

Winston Churchill took up his trademark V for Victory sign in public for the first time during a speech on 19 July 1941, even if he did go around for a few hours giving the wrong V sign to everyone until the error of his ways was pointed out by his secretary. The Aldwych V1 incident was one of the deadliest, leaving 34 dead and at least 200 injured, some seriously.

Powered by an Argus As 109-014 Pulsejet, the Vergeltungswaffe -1 (Vengeance Weapon 1) went into operational service on 12 June 1944, though all nine that were launched failed to reach England. However, it was a different story the following day when ten flying bombs were launched against London. Of these, four crashed on take-off, and two crashed into the Channel. Of the others, the first V1 to land in England hit the village of Swanscombe in Kent followed by hits on Bethnal Green, Sevenoaks and Cuckfield.

The V1 and subsequent V2 campaigns sparked off fresh rounds of evacuations including from Southampton. (George Greenwell, Daily Mirror).

Palmers Green station following a direct hit by a V2 rocket. The image, dated 7 November 1944, was taken by George Greenwell of the *Daily Mirror* using 35mm film. The edge of the impact crater is in the left foreground where the men are standing. (George Greenwell, *Daily Mirror*).

Waltham Abbey following a hit from a V2 on 7 March 1945. A fractured gas main proved a serious hazard to rescue operations (George Greenwell, *Daily Mirror*).

Daily Mirror

(MAY 8)

Tuesday, May 8, 1945
No. 12,911   ONE PENNY
Registered at G.P.O. as a Newspaper.

+ +

VE-DAY!

PUBLIC HOLIDAY TODAY AND TOMORROW—OFFICIAL

Massacre goes on in Prague as war ends

Soon after a Czech Spitfire squadron left Britain for Czechoslovakia yesterday large formations carrying Czechoslovak ground troops took off in the same direction. The commander, before leaving, said, "This is the greatest day of my life."

IN a final burst of fiendishness, S.S. troops in Prague last night were firing the last shots of the war on helpless Czech civilians.

S.S. men went through the streets driving people out of their homes as other S.S. troops waited to mow them down with machine-guns.

So bad has been the conduct of the German troops that the Wehrmacht commander of the area broadcast a warning to his men to respect international law.

"Some breaches," he actually admitted, had occurred.

But earlier he had announced that he did not recognise what he described as the "armistice."

"German troops will continue to fight until they have secured a free passage out of the country," he added.

According to refugees who have reached Pilsen the S.S. men, knowing that they will be executed when caught, have abandoned all normal conduct.

Another Prague broadcast reached Czechoslovak circles in London yesterday. It was an SOS from the Czechs pleading for speedy Allied help and asking "send us aircraft."

It spoke of heavy fighting in the streets, said the Germans were throwing hand grenades at houses showing Czechoslovak flags and reported the bombing by German planes of broadcasting house and other public buildings.

Meanwhile Patton's famous Fourth Armoured Division is speeding towards the capital and last night was reported to be fifteen miles south of the city.

War winners may broadcast today

The Prime Minister will broadcast at 3 p.m. today.

It is probable that later in the afternoon General Eisenhower, Field-Marshal Montgomery and Field-Marshal Alexander will also speak over the radio to the Allied world.

At 9 p.m. the King will broadcast.

NORWAY AWAITS ALLIED LANDINGS

An Allied naval force of forty-eight ships was reported yesterday at the entrance to Oslo Fiord, and troops are expected to land at any moment, according to Swedish reports.

Goebbels and his family are found, poisoned

DISCOVERY has been made in Berlin of the bodies of Dr. Goebbels, his wife, and their six children.

They were found by the Russians. All had taken poison and this was the cause of death.

Hitler's body has not been discovered and neither has the body of Goering.

There is now some speculation as to whether, after all, the Fuehrer and Goering may not have fled to a place of hiding.

It is pointed out, however, that their bodies may have been burned and the ashes lost in the wreckage of the burning Chancellery, or some other of Berlin's destroyed buildings.

★ **On top of the world**

In the heart of London an Allied soldier — he climbed the Eros statue in London's Piccadilly—gets just as high as he can to celebrate the lifting of the shadow from Europe.

Celebrations delay due to a 'technicality'

By BILL GREIG

THIS IS VE-DAY. AFTER FIVE YEARS, EIGHT MONTHS AND FOUR DAYS OF THE BLOODIEST WAR IN HISTORY BRITAIN AND HER ALLIES HAVE GAINED VICTORY IN EUROPE.

Capitulation of Germany to the Allies was announced by Doenitz yesterday—but a mere technicality in the arrangements made with Russia and America delayed the British people's celebration.

One result of the delay is that Britain's workers get two clear days' holiday—today and tomorrow. This Cabinet decision was disclosed last night.

Spend VE in camp, CO's say

"Daily Mirror" Reporter

COMMANDING officers of Army and RAF camps all over Britain told their men yesterday: "Spend VE-Day how you will, but PLEASE spend it in camp."

Thanksgiving services, concerts and later "closing time" for the canteen and sergeants' and officers' mess bars were some of the arrangements to persuade the men to stay in camp.

At an operational station near London the Daily Mirror was told by the Station Commander: "I have a lot of Australian air-crews here and they don't think VE day means the war is over as far as they are concerned. They've volunteered to forgo celebrations to do any odd job that comes up.

German prisoners of war have erected victory flag-poles at Catterick camp in North Yorkshire.

Originally it was intended that the first day's holiday would not begin until the Prime Minister had spoken.

The announcement late last night that today will be VE-Day was the final act in a bewildering day following the German surrender.

The people thronged out into the streets all over the country. In London there were thousands in Whitehall outside Downing-street patiently waiting for the word, little aware of the drama taking place inside No. 10.

There was chaos and bewilderment where there should have been celebration.

Here is the story of what happened in No. 10. When the news of the German surrender arrived the Prime Minister was ready to broadcast at 4 p.m. Hurried telephone calls were made to Marshal Stalin and President Truman so that the announcement could be made simultaneously.

Then it was that the trouble started. It was found that arrangements already made did not allow for the war ending so suddenly. Mr. Churchill put his broad-

Continued on Back Page

154

Victory and Beyond

On 23 May 1945, Prime Minister Winston Churchill resigned, forming a caretaker government until Parliament was dissolved on 15 June. Churchill dominated the Conservative campaign in the country's first general election since 1935, and though he had proved himself an excellent, if at times ruthless, wartime leader, he now proved something of a liability. During his first election broadcast he claimed an incoming Labour administration might form a British equivalent of the Gestapo.

The election was held on 5 July, though counting did not commence until 26 July to allow time for votes cast overseas to reach the UK. Labour won the election on a 9.7 per cent swing, taking 47.7 per cent of the popular vote, giving them 393 seats to the Tories 197. Churchill went to Buckingham Palace to tender his resignation in a chauffeur-driven Rolls-Royce, and incoming Prime Minister Clement Atlee turned up in a Standard Ten driven by his wife.

With the surrender of Japan in August 1945, those who expected life in the UK to quickly return to prewar conditions were in for a surprise. The US Government immediately pulled the plug on Lend-Lease hurling Britain's new Labour Government into crisis. The country was skint, the war had cost us £7.5 billion (£258.93 billion in 2019). Of this vast amount, overseas debt was about £3.3 billion, most of it owed to the United States. Austerity measures would have to remain in force for the foreseeable future.

On 27 June 1946, the government overreacted to a temporary fall in supplies of grain by doing something that had not been done even during the darkest days of the war. Bread was to be rationed from 21 July. The announcement was greeted in the Commons with tense silence. Winston Churchill described it as "one of the gravest I have ever heard in peacetime."

The adult ration was set at nine ounces (255 grams) of bread or flour a day, when at the time a whole loaf was usually fourteen ounces (397 grams) and more than many people already ate. There was an additional ration of up to fifteen ounces (425 grams) for male manual workers. Expectant mothers and women manual workers would get 11 ounces (312 grams), whilst at the other end of the scale, children under one year would get two ounces (57 grams). Bread rationing lasted until1948.

Food Minister John Strachey became the butt of numerous jokes and, even then, the Tories were

With the war in Europe fast concluding and the Luftwaffe no longer capable of mounting bombing raids, blackout restrictions were lifted. A well-lit café in Oxford Street, London, 23 April 1945. (John Heddon, *Daily Mirror*).

honing their three-word slogans with 'Starve with Strachey'. As it was, the public's faith in the rationing system was wearing thin, the upshot being the founding of the British Housewives' League by vicar's wife Mrs. Irene Lovelock. The League expressed the genuine feeling that people were sick to death of whinging politicians, austerity this, austerity that, and they were tired of being ordered around.

Within a few years of taking office, Labour had nationalised the railways, coal mines, utilities, airlines, and other key industries. On 5 July 1948, what is probably Labour's crowning glory came into being – the National Health Service. Minister of Health Aneurin Bevan stated that in its first full year the NHS would cost the country £249 million (£8,865,178,160. in 2019). Within twelve months the NHS had issued more than 200 million prescriptions, 4.5 million pairs of spectacles, and 8.5 million people had received free dental care. A concession to consultants was made that they could treat fee-paying clients in NHS hospitals rather than in private consulting rooms.

Housing was another post-war problem. Nationwide, only 200,000 new houses were completed during the war years, whilst by early 1946 more than 700,000 were still awaiting repair or demolition. The Housing Act, 1944, provided £150 million (£6.7 billion in 2019) to construct 250,000 homes on a temporary housing programme. The prefab was born. They were bolt-together single-storey homes that cost £40 (£1688 in 2019) each - more than a more traditional brick-built bungalow. But they did come complete with fixtures and fittings far beyond what many inner-city dwellers were used to such as flush toilets, fitted kitchens and wash boilers providing a constant supply of hot water. They even had a bit of garden. Desperate families took to squatting in abandoned military installations. Others were available to rent, such as the Nissen huts at Birch Hall Lane, Manchester, where rents ranged between 8s.3d (41p) and 11s.3d (56p) a week though the properties shared one cold water tap and there was no sanitation.

Then, on 28 August 1947, newspapers were reporting that the country was going back to a war footing with the introduction of super austerity. The main points were the banning of foreign holidays from 1 October, the meat ration was to be reduced from 1s 2d (6p) to one shilling (5p) from 7 September, and the basic petrol ration was to be abolished. Anyone staying in a hotel would now be required to surrender their ration book after two nights instead of the previous four nights, and hotels and restaurants would face a cut in food supplies of between fifteen and eighteen per cent. Works canteens would not be affected, neither would places charging not more than 2s 3d (11p) a head for a meal. On a positive note, the tea ration

VE Day at Buckingham Palace. Prime Minister Winston Churchill joins the Royal Family on the balcony. Left to right: Princess Elizabeth, Queen Elizabeth, Winston Churchill, King George VI, Princess Margaret. (Nixon & Greaves, *Daily Herald*).

remained at two ounces, expectant mums were to get an extra pint of milk a day together with extra eggs and an extra half ration of meat. They were also entitled to receive vitamins and concentrated orange juice and had priority for bananas and oranges as and when shipments arrived.

On the sporting front, the war ended too late for the Football League to return to its peacetime structure and, besides, many professional players were still serving with the armed forces. However, the FA Cup competition was restored and, for the only time in its history, all matches from the First Round Proper to the Sixth Round inclusive were played over two legs home and away.

The Sixth Round, Second Leg, also gave Britain its first football disaster of the postwar era. On 9 May, Bolton Wanderers were at home to Stoke City. Though a section of the ground was still in use as a storage facility by the War Department, officially 65,419 still managed to cram in, many gaining entry at the railway embankment end. However, many believe the gate was nearer to 85,000. Whatever the true figure was, 33 died and more than 400 were injured when just twelve minutes into the match two barriers collapsed, and the crowd fell forwards. The teams left the pitch. Half an hour later they returned and play continued, the dead put to one side and covered with coats. Blackpool skipper Stanley Matthews later said he was sickened that the game had been allowed to restart.

98.000 fans crammed into Wembley Stadium on 27 April to see Derby County play Charlton Athletic in the final. In the 85th minute, Bert Turner of Charlton Athletic scored an own goal then equalised in the 86th minute to put the game into extra time. It ended 4-1 to Derby County though, during the match, the ball had burst when Derby's centre forward Jack Stamps shot at goal. Five days later, when the two sides clashed in a South League match, the ball burst. It was said there was a gypsy curse on Derby County that they would never win the FA Cup whilst they played at the Baseball Ground. It is rumoured Jack Stamps paid a gypsy to lift the curse.

The Olympic Games returned in 1948. Held in London between 29 July and 14 August, they became known as the Austerity Olympics. There was no money to build new venues or an athletes'

village, so existing facilities were used, and competitors housed at military camps or in London colleges. Competitors were allowed increased rations up to 5467 calories a day, the same as mine workers. Interestingly, it was decided to retain the Olympic torch relay, first introduced by the Nazis in 1936.

During July 1948, flour was the first item to come off ration. The following year it was the turn of sweets, but they were put back on after just four months due to excessive demand. On 19 May 1950, canned fruit, jellies, mincemeat, syrup, treacle, and chocolate biscuits came off, and petrol followed at the end of the month due to a deal to pay some US suppliers in sterling. Christmas Day for children came on 5 February 1953, when once more sweets came off, even though sugar imports were still only 54 per cent of prewar levels. Food rationing finally came to an end after fourteen years on 4 July 1954, when restrictions on the sale of meat and bacon were lifted. For the first time since 1939, wholesale meat markets opened at midnight instead of 6.00 am. The demand for meat rocketed, resulting in the adoption of intensive rearing, especially for chickens. Production rose from five million in 1954 to 75 million in 1959.

Jubilant nurses in Liverpool celebrate VE Day. The Lord Mayor, Lord Sefton, announced the news from the Town Hall balcony. The celebrations carried on well into the night, thanks to a successful application by the Licensed Victuallers Association for a one-hour extension to pub opening times. They officially stayed open until 11.00pm, though there were city-wide lock ins. (*Liverpool Echo*).

VE Day celebrations around Piccadilly Circus. (Nixon & Greaves, *Daily Herald*).

VE Day revellers in Piccadilly Gardens, Manchester. At Trafford Park, there were scenes of confusion as hundreds of workers turned up to clock-on only to be told to go home. Many were under the impression that the VE Day national holiday did not begin until after Churchill's scheduled 3.00pm official broadcast on the BBC. By 10.00am, hundreds had gathered in Albert Square in anticipation of the raising of the flags of the 44 allied nations. However, they were in for a long wait as a town hall official declared the raising could not possibly take place until after Churchill's broadcast. (*Manchester Evening News*).

A scene played out in tens of thousands of streets. VE Day street party in full swing at Rosemary Lane, Lincoln. The flags and bunting were either left over from the end of World War One, or the coronation celebrations for King George VI. As to the food, rations were merged and American forces persuaded to part with some of their ample stores. 'Forgotten' items were suddenly 'rediscovered.' (*Lincolnshire Echo*).

VJ celebrations at Bridlington. (*Hull Daily Mail*).

Nigerian troops, camped in Kensington Gardens ahead of the 1946 Victory Parade, help one another to a dry shave. Representative units from the Allies took part except for the Polish. They were not invited for fear of upsetting Stalin. (*Daily Mirror*).

The RAF contingent at the 1946 Victory Parade held in London. (*Daily Mirror*).